CORINTHIAN
AND
ITALO-CORINTHIAN POTTERY
FROM THE POLISH COLLECTIONS

Στὴ μνήμη τοῦ
πατέρα μου

Universitas Iagellonica
Acta Scientiarum Litterarumque
DCCCLXXXIX
Schedae archaeologicae * Fasciculus XLIV

Studia ad Archaeologiam Mediterraneam pertinentia * Vol. X

EWDOKSIA PAPUCI-WŁADYKA

DE VASIS CORINTHIIS ET ITALO-CORINTHIIS IN COLLECTIONIBUS POLONORUM ASSERVATIS

Sumptibus Universitatis Iagellonicae

Zeszyty Naukowe
Uniwersytetu Jagiellońskiego
DCCCLXXXIX
Prace archeologiczne * Zeszyt 44

Studia z archeologii śródziemnomorskiej * Zeszyt 10

EWDOKSIA PAPUCI-WŁADYKA

CORINTHIAN AND ITALO—CORINTHIAN POTTERY FROM THE POLISH COLLECTIONS

Nakładem Uniwersytetu Jagiellońskiego

EDITOR OF ARCHAEOLOGICAL SERIES

Janusz K. Kozłowski

EDITOR OF VOLUME

Joachim Śliwa

REVIEWERS

Darrel A. Amyx (Berkeley)
Maria L. Bernhard (Warsaw)

TRANSLATION

Tomasz Podgórski

TECHNICAL EDITOR

Henryk Stachowski

PAŃSTWOWE WYDAWNICTWO NAUKOWE
ODDZIAŁ W KRAKOWIE UL. SŁAWKOWSKA 14
1354 ZESZYTY NAUKOWE UNIWERSYTETU JAGIELLOŃSKIEGO
DCCCLXXXIX PRACE ARCHEOLOGICZNE ZESZYT 44
NAKŁADEM UNIWERSYTETU JAGIELLOŃSKIEGO

Wydanie I. Nakład 705 + 80 egz. Ark. wyd. 8,75
Ark. druk. $4^{12}/_{16}$ + 22 wkładki. Oddano do składania w listopadzie 1988.
Podpisano do druku w lutym 1989 r.
Druk ukończono w marcu 1989 r.
Zam. 561/88   1005/89
SKŁADANO I ODBITO
W DRUKARNI UNIWERSYTETU JAGIELLOŃSKIEGO

ISBN 83-01-09349-8
ISSN 0083-4300

CONTENTS

1. INTRODUCTION

Among the Polish collections of Greek pottery, there is a considerable amount of vases coming from the workshops of Corinth and those Italic (mainly Etruscan), imitating original Corinthian production. Close research have revealed 138 vessels of this category [1]. Here come not only the objects from renowned National Museums, such as of Warsaw, Cracow and Poznań, but also those coming from minor collections, as yet many a time neither exhibited or published.

The lion's share of the objects under consideration (70 objects) remains in possesion of the National Museum in Warsaw [2]. In the post--war period, this Museum's Gallery of Ancient •Art has been enriched by the objects from the former Gołuchów collection (8 vases), objects from the Wilanów collection, accumulated by St. Kostka Potocki (5 items), and several vessels from the former Museum named after E. Majewski of Warsaw Scientific Society (3 objects). Part of the objects has been obtained by the Museum through revindication after the Second World War (46 vases). Another group comprises the objects acquired from the National Museum's own resources, or those coming from donations (8 items).

---

[1] Several objects had disappeared during the Second World War: two from Gołuchów collection — aryballos CVA Pologne 1, Pl. 6, 7a—b and alabastron Pl. 6, 9a—b; alabastron CVA Pologne 3, Pl. 2 (98) 7, aryballos ibid., Pl. 3 (119) 1, oinochoe ibid., Pl. 1 (122) 3. An aryballos passed for missing from Gołuchów collection, CVA Pologne 1, Pl. 7, 2, which has the shape of a warrior's head, and has been acknowledged by J. D. Beazley (JHS 52, 1932, p. 142) to be a Corinthian one; this vase has been since 1976 in Poznań (National Museum, inv. No. A 589) and is Rhodian, cf. Ducat, Les vases plastiques rhodiens, p. 71, No. 4. p, 156 „Groupe des élégants" dated 610—600; Kubczak, Katalog, No. 79, Fig. 34; Szymkiewicz, Studia Muzealne 14, 1984, p. 39, Fig. 14.

[2] Michałowski, Sztuka starożytna, p. 65ff.; Bernhard, p. 96—103.

A smaller collection, incuding 42 objects, is housed in several Cracow museums. The National Museum has 17 vases in Czartoryski Department [3], which are the objects from the former Czartoryski collection, objects from the former Museum of Technology and Industry, and the vessels obtained from donations. Quite a number of objects we are interested in here remains in possession of the Department of Mediterranean Archaeology of Jagellonian University (22 objects) [4]. On the other hand, the Archaeological Museum in Cracow has only 3 vases [5].

The third largest collection of Corinthian and Italo-Corinthian vases is to be found in Poznań. The National Museum there has 15 objects [6].

Several objects failing into the category considered here, completely unknown, come from the collections of minor museums. A smallish, yet very interesting collection is noterworthy, housed in the Museum at Cieszyn (8 objects) [7]. The Diocesan Museum in Płock has 3 objects [8].

The majority of objects, to which this work is devoted, had been earlier published by K. Bulas and M. L. Bernhard in *CVA Pologne* and other publications, and some had also been mentioned in specialistic works of such scholars as H. Payne (Nos. 17, 88), R. J. Hopper (Nos. 24—26, 39, 40, 52, 57, 66, 67, 88), D. A. Amyx (Nos. 56, 79, 88, 137), J. L. Benson (Nos. 39, 50, 78), J. Kubczak (Nos. 18, 23, 34, 64, 65, 95, 101, 117, 120, 125, 129, 137), J. Gy. Szilágyi (No. 138), A. Seeberg (Nos. 24—26). On the other hand, 20 objects were subject of the author's own studies, partly already published (Nos. 20, 27, 71, 77), partly announced for the first time in the present work (Nos. 5, 11, 45, 54, 55, 61, 62, 80, 81, 87, 102, 111, 112, 124, 135, 136).

As a long time has passed since the said objects had been rendered accessible, mainly through the publication in *CVA* (e.g. the Gołuchów vases or those from the Czartoryski collection in Cracow have not been studied for almost half a century), a comprehensive and more profound

---

[3] Sokołowski, *Muzeum XX Czartoryskich*, Kwartalnik Historyczny 6, 1892, p. 229—276; Komornicki, *Muzeum Książąt Czartoryskich*, p. 3—8; Bernhard, [in:] Rozprawy i Sprawozdania Muzeum Narodowego w Krakowie 10, 1970, p. 7—17; *Muzeum Narodowe w Krakowie, Zbiory Czartoryskich. Historia i wybór zabytków*, p. 5—45.

[4] Bernhard, *Katalog*, p. 9—18; Śliwa, *Zur Geschichte der Antikensammlung*, [in:] *Zur Geschichte der klassischen Archäologie Jena—Kraków*, p. 54—66.

[5] Bielenin, *XX-lecie działalności Muzeum Archeologicznego w Krakowie (1945—1963)*, Materiały Archeologiczne 6, 1965, p. 215.

[6] Kubczak, p. 161f.; Szymkiewicz, [in:] Kubczak, *Katalog*, p. 10ff.; id., Studia Muzealne, p. 29ff.; the vases from the former Ruxer collection are now stored as deposit at National Museum in Poznań (cf. Nos. 23, 101, 117).

[7] Brożek, [in:] Rocznik Muzeum Górnośląskiego w Bytomiu. Historia, fasc. 1, 1963, p. 15ff.

[8] The Płock objects have been in greater part acquired by Rev. L. Grabowski in the years 1950—1955 at Italian and Parisian antiquities' dealers, cf. Grabowski, *Muzeum Diecezjalne w Płocku. Informator*, p. 84f.

treatment is fully justified of Corinthian and Italo-Corinthian pottery. For instance, K. B u l a s in *CVA* made only the most general classification of vases, having not dated them and being not involved — in compliance with the then accepted guidelines of *CVA* — into the detailed stylistical and handiwork analyses. Since then, the studies on Corinthian pottery have made considerable progress. The latest excavations in the whole Mediterranean basin and in the Corinth itself have yielded new data and at times altered the hitherto dating of the said pottery. Also, studies greatly developed, aiming at an analysis of stylistical traits of figural representations in Corinthian vases, and at distinguishing the workshops and even artists, who had produced them. This concerns also Italo-Corinthian pottery. In this light, the Corinthian and Italo-Corinthian objects in Polish collections call for renewed examination.

As a result of our consideration, 52 vases have been placed for the first time within the frameworks of various groups, distinguished among Corinthian and Italo-Corinthian pottery, and their possibly exact dating has been forwarded (here come Nos. 2—5, 9—10, 12, 15—16, 19—22, 29, 32, 37—40, 42, 44, 47, 52, 53, 126—128, 130—134).

As far as 20 objects are concerned, the before settled classification or dating, or both these elements have been altered (Nos. 1, 17, 28, 34, 41, 43, 46, 48, 49, 51, 58, 60, 65, 85, 103, 113—117).

As a result of the detailed stylistical analysis of paintings in the discussed vases, several of them have been attributed to the previously known Corinthian painters. An oinochoe No. 14 represents intermediate style between the vases of Painter of Vatican 73 and these of Sphinx Painter. A round aryballos No. 27 was decorated by Bestum Painter. Such an analysis has also led to the distinguishing of the personages of the hitherto unknown Corinthian Painters, for which the conventional names have been proposed, "Painter of Seated Panther" and "Painter of Gołuchów Exaleiptron". The former adorned a round aryballos from Gołuchów collection, No. 30, whereas another made a painting on an exaleiptron No. 66, coming from the same collection. Another result of the said analysis is the rejection of the earlier forwarded attributions of some objects in our field of interest. The round aryballos No. 28 is here in question, which in this work's author's opinion, cannot be attributed to Warriors' Frieze Painter, likewise alabastron No. 68 is not the work of Cocks' Painter.

Finally, our consideration resulted in excluding several vessels from the circle of Corinthian art, which had formerly been tied to Corinthian workshops [9].

---

[9] The plastic vase in shape of hedgehog from Gołuchów coll., *CVA Pologne 1*, Pl. 7, 3, now in Warsaw, MNW 142407, is Rhodian (cf. D u c a t, *op. cit.*, p. 125f., type A, No. 1, group "Grenade I A", ca. 580); also the vase in form of shell,

Middle Corinthian, which embraces 28 vessels, opens with a large alabastron from the former Gołuchów collection, No. 40, decorated with a motif of four lotus flowers, and representing "white-dot-style". A similar motif encounter we on aryballoi Nos. 43—44. Another frequently occurring motif, decorating the vases of this shape, is a row of marching warriors with enormous shields, which started to appear already in Early Corinthian (No. 28), yet also unusually popular are in Middle Corinthian (Nos. 45—49). Several interesting vases place themselves in the final phase of Middle Corinthian. A flat-bottomed aryballos No. 50, representing probably Hermes, stylistically stands close to the Otterlo Painter (attribution by J. L. B e n s o n), whereas a round pyxis No. 56 is very near Geladakis Painter (attribution by D. A. A m y x). Another object, No. 66, illustrates the style of the above mentioned Painter of Gołuchów Exaleiptron. To the final stage of the discussed period belong also first published here pyxis No. 54, a broad--bottomed oinochoe No. 65 decorated by Saint Raymond Painter and amphora No. 67.

From the painters active in Late Corinthian I, the following are represented among ours collections: Winged Lion Painter (No. 78) and Herzegovina Painter (No. 79). From among 18 vases placing themselves within that phase of Corinthian vase painting, as many as 9 are quatrefoil aryballoi (Nos. 69—77), extremely popular in that time.

Then, in Late Corinthian II (17 vases), the most numerous vessels are exaleiptra (Nos. 92—99), of which the most interesting is provided with a foot (No. 99). This object boasts very diversified and carefully made decoration and come into being, according to A. G r e i f e n h a-g e n, in the same workshop as exaleiptra from Bonn and Heidelberg. Among the remaining vases from the discussed period, a round pyxis attracts attention with the handles in shape of female busts (No. 88), the only such a vase in Polish collections. This vase represents the white style and is dated to 545—525 B.C.

10 vases, Nos. 103—112, after all oinochoai of various type, place themselves within the frames of Classical period, embracing 5th and 4th centuries.

The last group of vases comprises Italo-Corinthian vessels, 26 in number (Nos. 113—138). Two currents can be distinguished among those objects. First of them, a linear one, is inspired by Protocorinthian and Early Corinthian pottery, from which it adopts the decorative idea based on a combination of bands and dots, at times also scale pattern (aryballoi Nos. 117—129, alabastra Nos. 130—136). To the same degree, Etruscan pottery production is stimulated by Corinthian animal style. Among our collections, this current is represented by only two vases: an alabastron No. 137 attributed by D. A. A m y x to the Tree Painter, and an olpe No. 138, which in opinion of J. Gy. S z i l á g y i is linked with Olpai Cycle, and according to M. L. Bernhard is the work of Queen's College Painter.

I would like to express my thanks to all those, who have contributed through their help to bringing this work into being. I owe my particularly warm thanks to Professor Maria L. Bernhard for her wholehearted care and support as well as for many a time manifested help and scientific supervision. I would also like to express my wholehearted thanks to Professor Darrel A. Amyx for his particular attenion and care in examining my manuscript, which resulted in numerous remarks, emendations and corrections I was able to introduce owing to Professor's kind helpfulness. I am especially obligated to Prof. Amyx for a possibility of making use of and quoting his work *Corinthian Vase-Painting of the Archaic Period*, not yet accessible and shortly to appear in print. I am grateful to Professor Olivier Picard, Director of École Française d'Archéologie at Athens, for his rendering possible my several months' stay in École, to Dr. Charles Williams, Director of American excavations in Corinth and to Dr. Nancy Bookidis, for making possible my stay in Corinth, rendering accessible the excavations' materials, and discussions on Corinthian art.

I also wish to acknowledge my debt to the Directors of respective Museums for their offering facilities to me in access to the objects and their consent on publication of those. My special thanks are owed to: Dr. Barbara Ruszczyc, Curator of the Gallery of Ancient Art, National Museum of Warsaw and the staff of this Gallery; Mrs. Krystyna Moczulska, M.A. Curator of the Department of Ancient Art, National Museum of Cracow; Dr. Hanna Szymańska-Wasylewska, Mediterranean Section, Archaeological Museum, Cracow; Mr. Jan Szymkiewicz, M.A., Curator of the Department of Ancient Art, National Museum, Poznań; Mrs. Małgorzata Płazak, M.A., Director of Museum in Cieszyn and Rev. Dr. Lech Grabowski, Director of Diocesan Museum, Płock.

I also wish to express my special thanks to Professor Joachim Śliwa, who encouraged, adviced and helped me many a time during my work on this publication.

2. CATALOGUE OF POTTERY

The particular items in the catalogue have been examined in keeping with the uniform schema, which comprises the basic data on a given object, that is the place where it is kept and its inventory number, the object's provenance (if known), its dimensions in metres (in turn: H = height, D = diameter), colour of clay and glaze, presence or lack of added paints and incisions, state of preservation of a given vase (only when the latter is damaged). Next, the object's bibliography is given; in case of the pots comprised in *CVA* their former publications have been omitted, except for those not given in the *Corpus*. A subsequent component of the catalogue note contains a detailed description of a given vase and its analysis, finally its classification and dating, and, where possible, determination of the stylistic group or the artist, to whom a given object could have been attributed. The numbers in plates correspond with the catalogue numbers of the vases. I realize that the figures in the plates should appear successively in keeping with their presentation in the *Catalogue* which is observed were possible (in compliance with a suggestion of Professor A m y x). This, however, was unfeasible in several instances due to technical reasons (dimensions of photographs).

Because of restrictions on space, it was necessary to use this in the most reasonable way. Thus, the vases' descriptions have been abbreviated to an indispensable minimum, and in the case of dates, the "B.C." has been consistently omitted. The names of museums, where the objects are being kept, have been given in an abbreviated form:

MAK — Muzeum Archeologiczne, Kraków (Archaeological Museum, Cracow);

MC — Muzeum w Cieszynie (Museum in Cieszyn);

MDP — Muzeum Diecezjalne, Płock (Diocesan Museum, Płock);

MNK — Muzeum Narodowe, Kraków (National Museum, Cracow);

MNP — Muzeum Narodowe, Poznań (National Museum, Poznań);

MNW— Muzeum Narodowe, Warszawa (National Museum, Warsaw);

NB — Nieborów (Nieborów, Department of Warsaw's National Museum);

ZAŚ UJ — Zakład Archeologii Śródziemnomorskiej Uniwersytetu Jagiellońskiego (Department of Mediterranean Archaeology of Jagellonian University, Cracow).

When quoting the publications, the initials of the authors' first names have been omitted, as have also been the places and years of editions, and in the case of the articles from periodicals, also titles of these. All those data are to be found in the list of abbreviations and in the bibliography, in the closing part of this work.

In consideration of the photographs, I am indebted to:

A. Wichniewicz: Cat. Nos. 4, 6—8, 10, 13—14, 17, 24—25, 28—29, 31, 33, 35, 38, 41, 43, 46, 49—51, 56, 58—60, 63, 68, 73, 74—78, 83—85, 90, 92—93, 97—100, 103, 106, 110, 113—116, 127, 138, (all from Warsaw National Museum's negatives);

K. Pollesch: Cat. Nos. 2, 3, 15—16, 19—22, 27, 32, 37, 42, 44, 47, 53, 67, 70—71, 77, 79, 86, 89, 91, 96, 105, 107, 111, 118—119, 121—123, 125—126, 128, 130, 132—134;

T. Biniewski: Cat. Nos. 1, 9, 11, 26, 30, 39, 48, 52, 57, 66, 69, 81, 94, 102, 108, 124, 135;

Z. Ratajczak: Cat. Nos. 18, 23, 34, 36, 40, 64, 65, 101, 117, 120, 129, 137;

D. Dubiel: Cat. Nos. 5, 54, 55, 61, 80, 109, 112;

M. Władyka: Cat. Nos. 45, 87, 136;

M. Drozdowski: Cat. No. 88.

2.1. GEOMETRIC

1. Oinochoe
Pl. I

MNW 142371 (Gołuchów coll.). Apulia. H: 0.29, D: 0.18. Yellow clay with red shade. Blackish-brown glaze, brownish-yellow in some places. Surface worn, some chips, crust on some spots. Bibliography: CVA Pologne 1, Pl. 6,1 (and the references there cited).

Broad-bottomed jar with a ring shaped foot, ovoid body, high cylindrical neck, massive trefoil mouth and band handle. On the neck, in rectangular panneau, ornament of seven zigzags between three lines. On the handle, horizontal bars. On the body, five groups of three reserved lines each. Bottom undecorated. Middle Geometric. 825—750.

Cf.: concerning the shape Corinth 7,1, p. 19, No. 70, Pl. 11 and p. 20, No. 71, Pl. 11; Corinth 13,1, p. 27, 18—2, Pl. 8 (= Coldstream, Greek Geometric

Pottery, Pl. 18b); similar decoration *Corinth 7,1*, p. 12, No. 33, Pl. 5; similar shape and decoration W e i n b e r g, *Hesperia* 17, 1948, p. 205, B2, B2, Pl. 71; similar oinochoai we also find among Attic pottery *CVA Copenhague 2*, Pl. 69, 6; K ü b l e r, *Kerameikos 5,1*, p. 233. Pl. 17-G 37; S m i t h s o n, Hesperia 43, 1974, Pl. 78, a-1, p. 362f.

2.2. PROTOCORINTHIAN

2. Skyphos   Pl. I

MNK XI-A-305. H: 0.081, D: 0.089 (with handles 0.125). Dark yellow clay with red shade. Red glaze, brown for rays. Missing: small part of rim. Bibliography: *CVA Pologne 2*, Pl. 1/94/3.

Slender, deep skyphos with a ring-shaped low foot. On the rim two lines, on handles: stripes. In the handle band, chevrons between groups of vertical bars. Below twelve stripes, rays at the bottom. Foot undecorated. Inside of vase covered by only partly preserved glaze. Middle Protocorinthian II. 690—670. Subgeometric style.

Cf.: B r o k a w, *Essays Carl Lehman*, p. 51f., Fig. 14—15; J o h a n s e n, p. 23f., Fig. 47, Pl. 17,2; D u n b a b i n, *Perachora 2*, p. 51, 53, No. 379, Pl. 19; V a l l e t, V i l l a r d, p. 38f.; similar are also: A l b i z z a t i, Pl. 1 : 8, 11; *CVA Oxford 2*, Pl. 1, 30; P a y n e, PV, Pl. 10; *CVA Louvre 13*, Pl. 36, 3—4; B o u c h e r, Cah. Byrsa 3, 1953, Pl. 2, 18, p. 15; *CVA Frankfurt a/M*, Pl. 13, 2; *CVA Turin 2*, Pl. 1, 3; *CVA Würzburg 1*, Pl. 30, 3—4.

3. Cup   Pl. I

MNK XI-A-198. H: 0.048, D: 0.105 (with handles 0.137). Light yellow clay. Brown glaze. Part of the mouth is missing. Bibliography: *CVA Pologne 2*, Pl. 1(94)4.

Deep cup with a conical foot, distinctly separated flaring mouth and two horizontal handles. Mouth glazed. The mouth-into-shoulders transition marked by a reserved line. In the handle band, vertical bars. On the body: broad band, glaze line and six rays. Glazed foot separated from the body by a reserved band. Middle Protocorinthian I and II. 690—650. Subgeometric style.

Cf.: concerning shape C a n c i a n i, AA, 1963, col. 556—566; parallels J o h a n s e n, Pl. 19,2; P a y n e, NC, p. 23, Fig. 9; V a l l e t, V i l l a r d, p. 36—38, Pl. 19,4; *CVA Oxford 2*, Pl. 1,23; *CVA Karlsruhe 1*, Pl. 38,2; B o u c h e r, Cah. Byrsa 3, 1953, p. 15, No. 17, Pl. 2.

4. Aryballos   Pl. II

Nb 1982 MNW. H: 0.06, D: 0.038. Yellowish clay. Mat glaze, yellow in some places. Glued together, restorations. Bibliography: *CVA Pologne 3*, Pl. 1/128/1.

Smallish conical vase with a flaring mouth, narrow, fairly high neck and flat shoulders. The neck decorated with bands and the shoulders with dot rosettes. On the body stripe and three broader bands. The conical aryballoi enjoyed popularity among the Protocorinthian ware in the first quarter of the 7th cent. Similar vases are to be found among the aryballoi from Perachora dated to that time. However, the discussed objects display more flat shoulders with their transition into body sharper, also the mouth is somewhat broader. Such properties point to the origin of the Nieborów object in the Middle Protocorinthian II. This dating is corroborated also by the inferior glaze quality. Middle Protocorinthian II. 670—650.

Cf.: D u n b a b i n, *Perachora 2*, p. 14, No. 23, Pl. 2, p. 19, No. 55, Pl. 3; D u g a s, EAD 10, Pl. 21, 137.

5. Aryballos   Pl. I

MC A 6/6 (donated by K n i c z e k 1846). H: 0.095, D: 0.056. Light yellow clay. Blackish-brown glaze, in some places reddish-yellow, lustrous. Added red (traces). Fragment of rim missing, decoration slightly worn off. Bibliography: unpublished.

Ovoid aryballos with a poorly separated foot, fairly flat shoulders, narrow, cylindrical neck and flat broad handle. On the mouth traces of dot rosettes (?) and red stripe. Handles edges glazed, in the middle vertical zigzag. On the shoulders, two figures of running dogs in silhouette technic, between those a zigzag. On the body five bands (their middle parts in added red), below seven narrow long rays. Foot glazed. On the bottom in the centre slight convexity, glazed. Middle Protocorinthian II. 670—650.

Cf.: D u n b a b i n, *Perachora 2*, p. 17, No. 30, Pl. 2 (shape), ibid. No. 29 (dogs on shoulders), ibid. No. 31 (dogs on shoulders, zigzag on handle).

6. Aryballos   Pl. III

MNW 199247 (1948, formerly in Königsberg). H: 0.066, D: 0.036. Buff clay. Black glaze. Added red. Incisions. Missing: rim and handle. On back side fracture and black stain. Bibliography: *CVA Pologne 5*, Pl. 12, 1—7 (and the references there cited).

Ovoid aryballos with short, ring-shaped foot and narrow cylindrical neck. On the neck, five vertical rows of dots with three dots in each. On the shoulders, intricate palmette and lotus pattern, made in outline technic. Below two bands, separated by triple lines. In the upper animal frieze: lion to r. between the bull (on the r.) and animal resembling the ass (on the l.), boar to r. opposite the capricorn, in the background three dot rosettes and ornament of hooked spirals. Careful and precise incisions, applied mainly for rendering the animal heads' details and partial outline accentuation. In the lower, five pin-wheel rosettes, interspersed with the ornament of hooked spirals. On the lower body, double series of rays. The ovoid body alongside such decoration properties as parting of individual decorative zones by triple lines, intricate ornament on shoulders made in outline technic, delicately proportioned animals not occupying the entire frieze height and incisions applied after all to the animals' heads, say for a dating this object to the Middle Protocorinthian. The figure of boar, decoration arrangement, filling ornament type and the shoulders' ornament put the said vase close to the two aryballoi, from Syracuse and Nola, decorated, according to Johansen and others, by the same artist. This painter has been named "Jägermaler" by Benson (= Huntsmen Painter of Amyx). Middle Protocorinthian II. 670—650.

Cf.: J o h a n s e n, p. 97, Nos. 42—43, Pl. 29; B e n s o n, GKV, p. 16, List 7; A m y x, Cor VP, p. 24, Nos. A-1, A-2.

7. Aryballos Pl. I

MNW 199246 (1948, formerly Königsberg). H: 0.071, D: 0.037. Buff clay with green shade. Black-brown glaze, rather mat, in greater part worn off. Bibliography: *CVA Pologne 5*, Pl. 11: 1, 4, 7; the object has been earlier published by L u l l i e s, p. 16, No. 22.

Pointed aryballos with a slender, narrow body, poorly separated foot, cylindrical neck, flat mouth, and massive bandhandle. On the mouth, two circles, on the handle three horizontal bars. Below the lower handle root, a stripe. On the upper body, seven densely distributed lines; on the lower body, five stripes more loosely spaced. On the bottom in the centre dot in circle. Late Protocorinthian. 650—630. Subgeometric style.

Cf.: *CVA Gela 1*, Pl. 9, 1 (with references).

8. Aryballos Pl. III

MNW 199248 (1948, formerly in Königsberg). H: 0.051, D: 0.031. Pale yellow clay. Brown glaze, in some places worn off. Missing: rim, neck and handle. The surface damaged. Bibliography: *CVA Pologne 5*, Pl. 11: 3, 6, 9 (and the references there cited).

Pointed aryballos with distinctly separated foot, body broad in its upper part and flat shoulders, decorated with tongues. The body decorated by two friezes of running dogs in silhouette technic, between three lines, below rays. Workmanship not very careful. Late Protocorinthian II. 650—630. Subgeometric style.

Cf.: D u n b a b i n, *Perachora 2*, p. 18, No. 44, Pl. 2 (there parallels); on running dog style J o h a n s e n, p. 78—79; P a y n e, NC, p. 8 n. 2, p. 74 n. 9; H o p p e r, p. 185—186; see also No. 37.

9. Aryballos Pl. III

MNW 142411 (Gołuchów coll.). H: 0.075, D: 0.04. Light yellow clay. Black lustrous glaze. Light brown in some places. Red and yellow added. Incisions. Bibliography: *CVA Pologne 1*, Pl. 6, 5 (and the references there cited).

Shape as No. 8. Decoration made in black polychrome technic. The entire vase is black. On the mouth, shoulders and on the lower body tongues done by incised strokes, which are alternately black, red and yellow. Red stripe on the handle. On the body, double scale-pattern made with compasses, embraced on both sides by a yellow stripe; on the scales, large red yellow dots. Transition from the body into the foot underlined with incised stroke. On the bottom in the centre, glazed cavity and a circle drawn around it. Late Protocorinthian — Transitional. 650—620.

Cf.: J o h a n s e n, p. 162f., Pl. 42, 2; P a y n e, NC, p. 286, Cat. No. 478; *CVA Gela 1*, Pl. 12, 2 (with many parallels); *Corinth 15, 3*, p. 75, No. 337, Pl. 17.

10. Skyphos   Pl. II

MNP A 723 (Gołuchów coll.). Carthage. H: 0.07, D: 0.085 (with handles 0.12). Light yellow clay with green shade. Black glaze, almost entirely worn off. One handle missing. Bibliography: *CVA Pologne 1*, Pl. 6, 2 (and the references there cited).

Shape similar to No. 2, yet more squat, with short ring-shaped foot. As indicated by traces, the inside, greater part of the body and the handles were glazed. On the lower body, well separated rays, coming from the line emphasizing the body-into-foot transition. On the bottom circles. Preserved traces of decoration indicate that the described vessel is the so-called black kotyle, known from the Protocorinthian and also manufactured in the Early Corinthian and even later. Late Protocorinthian — Early Corinthian. 2nd half of 7th cent.

Cf.: P a y n e, NC, p. 279, No. 201, p. 23, Fig. 9A, p. 309, Fig. 151, No. 973; *CVA Fogg Museum*, Pl. 4, 6; *Corinth 7, 1*, p. 59, No. 214, Pl. 24; *CVA Gela 2*, Pl. 24,3; *Corinth 7,2*, p. 124, An 133, Pl. 64; *Corinth 15,3*, p. 270, No. 1482.

11. Skyphos   Pl. I

MNW 143219 (deposit of Mr. Wołowski). H: 0.078, D: 0.082. Light yellow clay. There are not visible traces of glaze. Glued together, rim jagged, almost entire vase is covered by coarse brown-red colour crust. Bibliography: unpublished.

Deep thin-walled skyphos with a fairly massive foot and two horizontal handles just below the rim. Slight narrowing just above the foot, walls bulged and in the uppermost portion somewhat inwards-inclined. The state of preservation of the vase in question considerably hampers its classification and dating. Its clay could have indicated on its origin in a Corinthian workshop. Slender shape and narrow foot say for an early dating, since the later skyphoi are more squat, have broad foot and almost straight walls (cf. Nos. 59—61). It should be stressed, however, that the profil of the skyphos cannot serve as an exact dating criterion (cf. D u n b a b i n, *Perachora 2*, p. 240, p. 52 Fig. 1). Protocorinthian — Early Corinthian?

Cf.: concerning Corinthian skyphoi P a y n e, NC, p. 294—295; H o p p e r, p. 221; see also No. 2.

2.3. TRANSITIONAL

12. Aryballos

Pl. III

MNW 198539 (1946, formerly Wrocław Museum). H: 0.098, D: 0.052. Light yellow clay. Black lustrous glaze, effaced in upper part. Red added. Incisions. Bibliography: *CVA Pologne 5*, Pl. 11: 2, 5, 8.

Shape similar to No. 9, but stronger narrowing in the lower body part, the foot is lacking. On the mouth, shoulders and lower body tongues. On the handle zigzag, its edges glazed. On the body a broad band of the scale pattern (double incised strokes made with compasses, red dots within the scales), framed on both sides by double stripes. On the bottom, dot enclosed by a circle, which embraces also the lower portion of the body. Transitional. 630—620.

Cf.: J o h a n s e n, p. 162, Pl. 42, 1; P a y n e, NC, p. 22, Fig. 8A, p. 23, 26, 286, No. 478A; U r e AFR, p. 20; D u n b a b i n, *Perachora 2*, p. 19, No. 48; L o P o r t o, p. 48f., Fig. 33a, 34a; *Corinth 13, 1*, Pl. 12: 78—3; *CVA Gela 1*, Pl. 12, 3—5, Pl. 1—3 (there parallels); *Corinth 15, 3*, p. 76, No. 339, Pl. 17.

13. Alabastron

Pl. III

MNW 199237 (1948, formerly Königsberg). H: 0.071, D: 0.047; Light rosy clay. Black-brown glaze, almost entirely worn off. Traces of red-violet added. Incisions. Missing: rim, handle and neck, the rest glued together. Bibliography: *CVA Pologne 5*, Pl. 13, 1—5 and Fig. 1 (and references there cited).

Vase with a squat body and slightly flattened bottom, decorated with the antithetic group of lion and bull with a hare between them. In the background, dot-in-circle rosettes and dots. On the bottom, a rosette made of large dots. Transitional. 630—620.

Cf.: concerning the dot-in-circle rosette L o P o r t o, p. 7f.; the motif of lion opposing bull is frequent on alabastra of Ardea Painter (on whom see *CVA Gela 1*, Pl. 15); this motif also on alabastron in Palermo: T u s a, ASAtene 44, 1982, p. 195, Fig. 6, p. 200 (from Selinus).

14. Oinochoe

Pl. IV

MNW 138518 (1946, formerly Szczecin). H: 0.18, D: 0.20, Buff clay. Black lustrous glaze, partly worn off. Red added. Incisions. Missing: almost whole rim, handle, part of neck, part of body (restored). Bibliography: *CVA Pologne 5*, Pl. 14, 1—4 and 15; A m y x, CorVP, p. 70, No. B-4.

Broad-bottomed oinochoe with a squat body and broad low neck. The preserved fragment of neck and mouth: black. Below, two animal friezes, parted by a band of dots in chequered pattern between triple red lines. Upper frieze: in the middle swan to r. between two seated sphinxes (that on the right partially preserved fragment of neck and mouth: black. Below, two animal friezes, parted by a band of dots in chequered pattern between triple red lines. Upper frieze: in the middle swan to r. between two seated sphinxes (that on the right partially preserved), left to the group, panther to r. and swan to l., right to the group there were probably also two animals, of which a boar to r. has partially survived. Lower frieze: in the centre boar to r. between lion and panther, on the left: group of a boar to l. between the two panthers; on the right: group of a bull to l. between lion and panther. Red applied on the birds' wings and on the animals' necks and bodies. Incisions made carefully and skillfully. On the vessel's bottom there is a groove. The style of paintings on the oinochoe under consideration resembles the technic of both Painter of Vatican 73 and Sphinx Painter, yet cannot be acknowledged as a work of either, considering the differences. This is also the opinion of Professor Amyx (see the bibliography above). Transitional. 630—620. Stylistically between Painter of Vatican 73 and Sphinx Painter.

Cf.: concerning the shape J o h a n s e n, Pl. 19, 3; P a y n e, NC, p. 299, 315, 325; another variety of this shape is No. 63; on Painter of Vatican 73: P a y n e, NC, p. 277; A m y x, AJA, 70, 1966, p. 296; V a l l e t - V i l l a r d, p. 51, Pl. 53, Pl. 33: 2, 3, 5, 8, Pl. 37: 1—5; CVA Louvre 13, p. 51—55 (Villard); B e n s o n, GKV, p. 25, List 28 (Sphinx Maler); H o f f m a n, JbHambKuSamml 8, 1963, p. 214f.; K u n i s c h, Antiken der Sammlung Julius C. und Margot Funcke, p. 36, No. 40; L u l l i e s, Antike Kunstwerke der Sammlung Ludwig, 1, p. 32f., Nos. 10, 11; H o l m b e r g, P a s q u i e r, Op. Ath 15, 1984, p. 52—54; on Sphinx Painter: A m y x, op. cit.; Corinth 7, 2, p. 17, under No. 17 (A m y x, L a w r e n c e).

15. Pyxis Pl. II

MAK AS/3591. Panticapaion. H: 0.043, D: 0.08, D lid: 0.088. Buff clay, clay of lid is yellowish-grey. Black mat glaze. Red and white added. Incisions. One handle broken off, lid glued together decoration slightly worn off. Bibliography: CVA Pologne 2, Pl. 4/93/4; P a p u c i, RechACrac 1977, p. 59f., Fig. 2: A (without lid).

This vase has been published without a lid. However, recently the lid has been found in the collection of Department of Mediterranean Archaeology of Jagellonian University, which regarding dimentions and decoration, fits very closely to the box of the pyxis and surely belonged to it. The pyxis is cylindrical with concave sides, fitted with two horizontal handles; the lid is flat with a moulded lug. A very plain decoration comprises black and red lines, as well as dots; in the main band on the pyxis' walls and on the surface of the lid there is a "triglyph--motope" pattern, exposed by double incised strokes with white dot rosettes in the "metopes". Transitional — Early Corinthian. 630—590. Linear decoration, band-and-dot style.

Cf.: on shape CVA Gela 1, Pl. 2; on lid H o p p e r, p. 207—208; D u n b a b i n, Perachora 2, p. 175, 183, No. 1882, 3; CVA Tübingen 1, Pl. 27, 11—12, p. 55, Fig. 18 (similar shape); L o P o r t o, p. 117, complesso 58, 3, Fig. 92b (similar decoration, but convex sides); V a l l e t, V i l l a r d, Pl. 38, 13, p. 55 (similar main band).

2.4. EARLY CORINTHIAN

16. Alabastron   Pl. IV

MNK XI-1063 (Czartoryski coll.). H: 0.085, D: 0.05. Buff clay. Black semi--lustrous glaze. Red added. Incisions. Bibliography: *CVA Pologne 2*, Pl. 3/57/2; P a p u c i - W ł a d y k a, No. 4.

Alabastron of small dimentions. On the mouth, neck and bottom tongues. Dots on the rim. On the handle: vertical stroke. On the body, in antithetic arrangement, bird with the panther's head and siren with a high polos on the head. Careful workmanship. Early Corinthian. 620— 590. Group A of Small alabastra in Payne's classification.

Cf.: P a y n e, NC, p. 281f., No. 208ff and p. 90; on motif of panther-bird see B e n s o n, AJA, 68, 1964, p. 171 n. 47; *CVA Gela 1*, Pl. 34, 1—4; motif of two panther-birds opposing D u g a s, EAD 10, Pl. 29, 404 (= P a y n e, NC, No. 309).

17. Alabastron   Pl. VII

MNW 199236 (1948, formerly in Königsberg). H: 0.081, D: 0.049. Pale yellow clay. Black lustrous glaze. Red added. Incisions. Missing: rim and greater part of handle. Bibliography: P a y n e, NC, p. 283, No. 354; L u l l i e s, No. 18; *CVA Pologne 5*, Pl. 27, 1—3; B e r n h a r d, Fig. 169; L a w r e n c e, AJA 63, 1959, p. 357 n. 18. (I owe this reference to Prof. Amyx.)

Small alabastron. The neck and the bottom of the vase decorated by tongues. On the preserved handle fragment, traces of a vertical bar. On the body representation of two horses' protomes with fore legs, in antithetic arrangement; the hind quarters of the horses have the shape of birds' tails. Incisions are rich and skilfully done, some parts of contours are underlined with incised lines (e.g. snouts and legs). Added paints occur on the horses' shoulders. In the background, incised rosettes. Careful workmanship. Early Corinthian. 620—590. Payne's group A of small alabastra.

Cf.: antithetic harses' protomes: D u n b a b i n, *Perachora 2*, p. 143, No. 1528, Pl. 59, p. 197, No. 1965, Pl. 62; L a w r e n c e, loc. cit.; G j e r s t a d, *Greek Pottery*, p. 40, No. 350, Pl. 25, 7; S i e v e k i n g - H a c k l, p. 31, Fig. 46 (= P a y n e, NC, No. 1047); *CVA Louvre 6*, Pl. 7, 9—11 (= P a y n e, NC, No. 1406); concerning animals' protomes on Corinthian vases: *CVA Heidelberg 1*, Pl. 9, 5—7 (Schauenburg).

18. Alabastron   Pl. IV

MNP A 11 (formerly Antiquarium, Berlin). Smyrna. H: 0.09. D: 0.05. Light yellow clay with green shade. Glaze almost entirely worn off. Purple added. Small chips on surface. Bibliography: *CVA Pologne 3*, Pl. 3/119/5; K u b c z a k, p. 164, Fig. 4; id., *Katalog*, No. 72.

Small alabastron. On the surface of the mouth and on the neck tongues. On the rim traces of dots. Handle glazed. The body adorned by the representation of a siren with widespread wings going to l. and with head turned back (purple applied on face and wings). Filling ornament: two stylized lotus flowers at the siren's head, incised rosettes rosette-flower with a double circle in the centre, triangular spot with incised triangle inside. Early Corinthian, Beginning of 6th cent. Payne's group A of small alabastra.

Cf.: P a y n e, NC, p. 282, No. 327ff; similar siren in round aryballos CVA Gela 1, Pl. 36.

19. Alabastron   Pl. IV

ZAŚ UJ 10.174 (donated by W. Czartoryski, 1872), H: 0.085, D: 0.045. Buff clay. Blackish-brown glaze. Glued together, small injuries. Bibliography: CVA Pologne 2, Pl. 5/78/10; B e r n h a r d, Katalog, No. 306; P a p u c i - W ł a d y k a, No. 4.

Small alabastron. On the mouth red circle, on the rim stripe. On the handle horizontal bars. Neck decorated by the tongues ornament. The body's decoration comprises bands and dots. Early Corinthian 620—590. Linear style.

Cf.: our alabastron is another version of vase illustrated in P a y n e's Fig. 121 bis, NC p. 284, No. 377; CVA Gela 1, Pl. 19, 1—3 (with many parallels); Corinth 15, 3, p. 286, No. 1556, Pl. 63.

20. Alabastron   Pl. IV

MNK XI-A-346 (donated by A. Schmaus). H: 0.075, D: 0.04. Buff clay. Blackish-brown glaze. Missing: part of the mouth; decoration heavily worn off. Bibliography: P a p u c i - W ł a d y k a, No. 2.

Shape similar to the former, more slender. On the preserved fragment of the mouth concentric circles. On the handle vertical strip. On the body, traces of band decoration with one broader band filled with dots. Classification and dating as No. 19.

21. Alabastron   Pl. IV

ZAŚ UJ 10.176 (donated by W. Czartoryski, 1872). H: 0.075, D: 0.045. Dark yellow clay. Brownish-red glaze. Decoration heavily worn off. Bibliography: CVA Pologne 2, Pl. 5/78/1; B e r n h a r d, Katalog, No. 304; P a p u c i - W ł a d y k a, No. 3.

Shape similar to No. 19, more squat. Decoration as in the case of No. 19, as well as classification and dating.

22. Alabastron   Pl. III

ZAŚ UJ 10.175 (donated by M. Bodeńska). H: 0.075, D: 0.045. Buff clay. Blackish-brown glaze. Decoration heavily worn off. Rough surface. Bibliography: CVA Pologne 2, Pl. 5/78/7; B e r n h a r d, Katalog, No. 200; P a p u c i - W ł a d y k a, No. 20.

Small alabastron with fairly broad neck and smallish handle with horizontal bars visible on the latter. On the neck traces of tongues. Body decorated with steadily distributed stripes. This vase has been formerly classified by me with the Italo-Corinthian pottery, yet as a result of another analysis of the object I would rather recognize it as the product of Corinthian workshops. The vase represents the alabastron type similar to the object No. 19, but devoid of bands filled with dots. Early Corinthian. 620—590. Linear style.

Cf.: P a y n e, NC, p. 283, Fig. 121 B, p. 284, No. 376 A, group C I; P e r d r i z e t, FdD 5, Fig. 612 - 613; D u g a s, EAD 10, Pl. 29, No. 375—377; B o u c h e r, Cah. Byrsa 3, 1953, Pl. 4, 39; L o P o r t o, p. 56, Fig. 40 b; G j e r s t a d, *Greek Pottery*, p. 40, No. 351, Pl. 25; *Corinth 15, 3*, p. 285, n. 1.

23. Alabastron Pl. IV

MNP deposit 1091 (ex Ruxer coll.). H: 0.095, D: 0.055. Light yellow clay. Brownish-black lustrous glaze. Missing: fragment of rim and neck. Decoration heavily worn off. Bibliography: *CVA Pologne 3*, Pl. 1/122/5; K u b c z a k, p. 165, Fig. 5.

Squat alabastron with a broad neck and massive handle. On the mouth three circles. On the handle, two large dots. On the the neck tongues. On the body, three broad bands alternately with six narrower ones, coupled. On the bottom, in the central part, there is the cavity. Careless workmanship. The vase — if we acknowledge it being a Corinthian product, which is supported by light clay, fairly broad neck and the fact that the tongues do not transgress the lower handle root — represents the same alabastron type with a linear decoration as formerly described, yet displays bands of different width.

24. Alabastron Pl. V

MNW 147184 (St. K. Potocki coll., formerly in Wilanów). H: 0.213, D: 0.115. Buff clay with green shade. Blackish-brown glaze, in some places worn off. Dark violet for many details. Incisions. Mouth slightly jagged. Bibliography: *CVA Pologne 3*, Pl. 1/113/1; B e r n h a r d, Meander 6, 1951, p. 436, Fig. 4; H o p p e r, p. 193, 8; M i c h a ł o w s k i, *Sztuka starożytna*, p. 96, Fig. 48; S e e b e r g, ActaA 35, 1964, p. 36—38, Fig. 17—18 (details); B e r n h a r d, Fig. 166; A m y x, CSCA 2, 1969, p. 17—18; S e e b e r g, CorKV, p. 35, No. 189a and p. 62; D o b r o w o l s k i, Biuletyn Historii Sztuki 34, 1972, p. 171, Fig. 2; A m y x, CorVP, p. 115, No. A-1; see also: stamp 1 zł, Polish Mail, 1976 (special issue for Postage Stamp Day), fantastically being from the upper frieze.

Alabastron of a big size. On the concave mouth, neck and the vase's bottom tongues. On the handle vertical stripe. The body is occupied by two friezes separated by two stripes, and framed above and below by three stripes. Upper frieze: in the middle winged figure — Artemis? — (hair-band, long robe) holding two swans by neck; left to this, a fantastical being and swan. Lower frieze: a padded dancers in closely fitting tunics; six bearded make a "chorus" with one of them facing r., opposit him five dancers are visible in a row, while the two remaining dancers in the frieze have no beards and are shown facing each other. Dancer on the r. turns on another with a mace. In the background of both friezes, dense filling ornament: incised rosettes, rosettes with a single or double circle inside, glaze spots assuming the shape of free space and dots. The above described alabastron and similar to it, although bearing different decorative motifs, alabastron No. 25, are the works of the same hand, the so-called Wilanów Painter. The attribution and the establishment of name for this anonymous Corinthian painter have been done by American scholar D. A. Amyx, who drew attention of Norwegian A. Seeberg to the Warsaw vases. Seeberg has done further attributions to Wilanów Painter and ascertained him to be one of the painters specializing in representations of the grotesque dancers. According to Prof. Amyx to this hand also belong alabastra Eton College Museum and Madrid 32647 (A m y x, CorVP, p. 215, Nos. A-3, A-4) and related is Basel Market MuM Auktion 26 (1963), p. 33, Pl. 21, No. 67 (this vase later is Milwaukee No. 11606 — Painter of Stockholm 1654, A m y x, CorVP, p. 153, No. A-2). Wilanów Painter has been the close co-worker of another komasts' specialist, Wellcome Painter. Both these artists trace their origin back to the so-called Warrior Group. Early Corinthian. Ca 600. Wilanów Painter (Amyx, Seeberg).

Cf.: bibliography of item; on Warrior Group A m y x, CSCA 2, 1969, p. 1—25,

25. Alabastron
Pl. VI

MNW 147185 (St. K. Potocki coll., formerly Wilanów). H: 0.215, D: 0.107. Buff clay with green shade. Blackish-brown glaze, brownish-orange in some places. Dark violet for many details. Incisions. Mouth slightly jagged. Bibliography: CVA Pologne 3, Pl. 1/113/2; H o p p e r, p. 193, 8; B e r n h a r d, Meander 6, 1951, p. 436, Fig. 3; S e e b e r g, Acta A, loc. cit.; A m y x, op. cit.; S e e b e r g, CorKV, p. 35; D o b r o w o l s k i, op. cit., p. 171, Fig. 1; A m y x, CorVP, p. 115, No. A-2.

Large-sized alabastron. Disposition of the decoration and ornaments as in the case of No. 24. Upper frieze: group of a seated lion to r. opposite the panther, between them, a floral ornament — palmette and lotus flower; below the handle swan to l. with raised wings. Lower frieze: a comically treated group attracts attention of a man leaning against the spear (hair-band, beard, greaves) and a hare standing up before him on its hind legs, and hilding out its fore paws towards the man as if begging for something; two stout bulls attacking one another. Added paints traditional. Early Corinthian. Ca 600. Wilanów Painter (Amyx, Seeberg).

Cf. No. 24.

26. Alabastron
Pl. VII

MNW 142372 (Gołuchów coll.). H: 0.30, D: 0.15. Cream-coloured clay. Black

glaze. Red for many details. Incisions. Bibliography: *CVA Pologne 1*, Pl. 6, 11
(and the references there cited); H o p p e r, p. 193, 7; B e n s o n, GKV, p. 118,
No. 369; S e e b e r g, Acta A 35, 1964, p. 46; id., CorKV, p. 23, No. 75, p. 59;
A m y x, CorVP, p. 117, No. B-3.

Alabastron of a large size. On the mouth and the bottom tongues
embraced by circles. On the rim a pattern comprising elements resembling the "z". Handle glazed. On the neck long tongues. The body
is occupied by three friezes, separated by several lines, which show
bearded padded dancers in identical attitude, to r. (red added on beards
and chitons). In the upper frieze five, in the middle seven and in the
lower nine komasts. Dense filling ornament: rosettes and dots. A whole
series of vases is concentrated around the above mentioned (cf. No. 24)
Wellcome Painter, the Wellcome Sequence in a classification forwarded
by Seeberg. Wellcome Painter was also the head of Wellcome Workshop, which had specialized in mass production of cheap vases with
the representations of lined-up komasts. According to Seeberg, one of
this workshop's products is the alabastron under consideration. An early
phase of Wellcome Painter and of whole Sequence falls to the last
years of Early Corinthian, whereas the end of production takes place
several years before the end of Middle Corinthian. Ca 600. Wellcome
Workshop (Seeberg). According to Prof. Amyx this vase stands "Near
the Altenburg Painter".

27. Aryballos   Pl. VIII

ZAŚ UJ 10.333. H: 0.051, D: 0.048. Buff clay. Black glaze, in some places
blackish-brown. Red for details. Incisions. Missing: fragment of rim and small
part of body. Decoration worn off. Bibliography: P a p u c i - W ł a d y k a, No. 8;
ead., RechACrac 1983, p. 70—72, Fig. 1; ead., Meander 40, 1985, p. 193—194, Fig. 1.

Round aryballos. On the mouth traces of circles, on the rim remains
of large dots. On the handle three horizontal bars. On the shoulders
tongues, below two lines. On the body frieze of four padded dancers
(three figures preserved). On the bottom circles. Dancers to r., worn in
tight-fitting tunics with added red. In the frieze background incised
rosettes. The already described Cracow object was adorned by the hand
of an anonymous artist, named Bestum Painter, who used to specialize
in decorating the round aryballoi with the representations of kômoi.
This painter belongs to the mentioned Wellcome Sequence (cf. No. 26)
together with Wellcome Painter and his workshop, Altenburg Painter
and others. Seeberg attributed to Bestum Painter 11 vases and fragments. In my opinion, the Cracow object can be added as the 12th
to that list. Early Corinthian. Late phase. Bestum Painter.

28. Aryballos   Pl. IX

MNW 198023 (1946, formerly Wrocław). H: 0.064, D: 0.068. Light yellow clay.
Brownish-black glaze, in some places brownish-red. Violet for details. Incisions.

Missing: rim and handle. Glued together, partly restored, surface damaged, crust in some places. Bibliography: *CVA Pologne 5*, Pl. 36, 1—3 (and the references there cited); B e r n h a r d, Fig. 171.

Round aryballos with a slightly flattened body. On the shoulders long tongues, below three lines. On the body frieze of five warriors marching to l. Their heads are treated in the same manner as those of padded dancers: lines render eyes, mouths, ears, and hair-bands. Four warriors are bearded, one beardless wears a helmet. They are screened by enormous shields (incised zigzags enclosed in two circles at their rims, central parts in added colours and in two cases additionally decorated). The space between warriors is filled with large dots, on the back below the handle there was probably some kind of ornament (a small cross in the upper part has survived). On the bottom eight concentric circles, one close to another. The aryballoi with the motif of marching warriors appear in Early Corinthian and had been enjoying popularity during the first 30 years of the 6th cent., displaying more and more schematization and degeneration of the drawing technic. Since the decoration of the Warsaw aryballos is relatively careful (cf. e.g. later aryballos No. 49), the warriors bear the numerous details marked, ornaments occur on the shields and the representation's background, the discussed object should be placed within the group IV, VI. b in the Ure's classification of the aryballoi from Rhitsona. Early Corinthian. Late 7th — early 6th cent.

Cf.: U r e, AFR, p. 23 and 38; see also Nos. 45—49.

29. Aryballos

Pl. XI

MNW 138004 (formerly E. Majewski coll.). Kume. H: 0.067, D: 0.06. Buff clay. Blackish-brown glaze. Red applied. Incisions. Rim, neck and fragment of handle modern. Decoration partly worn off. Bibliography: *CVA Pologne 3*, Pl. 2/98/5; B e r n h a r d, *Wazy greckie w Muzeum im. E. Majewskiego WTN w Warszawie*, p. 4—5, Pl. 1, 5—6.

Aryballos with almost perfectly round body. The handle edges were glazed and a zigzag runs through its middle part. On the body, deer to r. (added paint on neck and abdomen). Thickstroked incisions made carefully. In the background incised and dot-in-circle rosettes. On the bottom rosette made of large dots. Early Corinthian. Early phase.

Cf.: no exact parallels; on motif of deer on aryballoi P a y n e, NC, p. 290, Nos. 564ff.; D u g a s, EAD 10, Pl. 24, Nos. 268—270; Laurens, p. 83ff., Nos. 29—30.

30. Aryballos

Pl. X

MNW 142409 (Gołuchów coll.). H: 0.07, D: 0.07. Yellowish clay. Black glaze, in some places worn off. Dark violet for details. Incisions. Missing: part of mouth (restored). Surface damaged. Bibliography: *CVA Pologne 1*, Pl. 6, 6 (and the references there cited); A m y x, CorVP, p. 126, No. 3.

Round aryballos with a slightly flattened body. On the concave mouth a circle. On the shoulders short tongues. Handle decorated with horizontal bars. On the body representation of the seated panther to r. with long, fancifully crooked tail. In the background: incised rosettes, rosettes with double circle inside. Almost identical representation of panthers we encounter on the two aryballoi from Louvre, A 447 and A 448, and on an aryballos from Jalyssos (Rhodos). All the four aryballoi display far-reaching similarities in composition of representations, stylistic traits of drawing and filling ornament, which enable their recognition as works of the same hand. I propose their anonymous artist to be named Painter of Seated Panther. Prof Amyx calls the artist "Painter of the Pendant Panthers". A panther similar to that on the Warsaw object is also to be found on an aryballos from Carthage, whose decoration is so strongly worn off that it renders impossible a more profound comparison. Early Corinthian. 620—590. Painter of the Seated Panther.

Cf.: *CVA Louvre 8*, Pl. 18, 1—6. 10. 12; Cl. Rh. 3, Jalyssos gr. 46, 7, p. 79f., Fig. 70, Pl. 7 (= *CVA Rhodi 2*, Pl. 8, 6); B o u c h e r, CahByrsa 3, 1953, Pl. 7, 55, p. 22 (from Carthage); detailed study concerning the Painter of the Seated Panther is being prepared for publication by the author of the present work.

31. Aryballos   Pl. XI

MNW 199242 (1948, formerly probably in Königsberg). H: 0.05, D: 0.052. Light yellow clay with green shade. Traces of blackish-brown glaze and added red. Incisions. Missing: fragment of mouth. Very damaged: glued together, partly restored, surface effaced. Bibliography: *CVA Pologne 5*, Pl. 33, 2, and 30, 2.

Round aryballos with a short neck and broad mouth. On this traces of circles. On the shoulders tongues. On the front part of the body bird with widespread wings to l., standing on a half of a petal rosette. In the background incised rosettes. The representation of a bird with spread wings, called conventionally the "swan", ranks among favourite decorative motifs on round aryballoi in Early Corinthian. The closest to the bird on the Warsaw aryballos are representations on aryballoi from Delos. Early Corinthian. 620—590.

Cf.: P a y n e, NC, p. 290, No. 585 (aryballos from Corinth there cited has been published: *Corinth* 7, 2, p. 21, No. 36, Pl. 6); D u g a s, EAD 10, Pl. 23, Nos. 236—238 and 241; *CVA Gela 1*, Pl. 28, 1—4 (with many parallels); see also No. 32.

32. Aryballos   Pl. X

MNK XI-1415 (Czartoryski coll.). H: 0.058, D: 0.056. Buff clay. Blackish-brown glaze. Red applied. Incisions. In upper part of body decoration worn off. Bibliography: *CVA Pologne 2*, Pl. 3/57/3; G ą s i o r o w s k i, *Malarstwo starożytne*, Pl. 2a; P a p u c i - W ł a d y k a, No. 5.

Round aryballos. On the neck and shoulders tongues; on the rim dots. On the handle zigzag between vertical bars. On the body swan with widespread wings standing on a half of petalled rosette. Below the handle quadrilateral rosette within a circle and four such rosettes out of it. Early Corinthian. 620—590.

Cf.: classification as No. 31; *CVA Bibliothèque National 1*, Pl. 14, 13 (similar bird); D u g a s, EAD 10, Pl. 23, 229—228 (similar motif below handle); according to Prof. Amyx close is also aryballos S i e v e k i n g - H a c k l, No. 300.

33. Aryballos Pl. XI

MNW 199244 (1948, formerly Frombork). H: 0.045, D: 0.055. Whitish clay. Black (brown in some places), semilustrous glaze. Reddish-violet for details. Incisions. Missing: mouth, neck and handle. Surface damaged, small chips. Bibliography: *CVA Pologne 5*, Pl. 33, 3—6.

Round aryballos with a flattened body. On the shoulders, large dots. On the bottom petalled rosette around an incised circle. On the body representation of a lion and swan facing each other. In the background incised rosettes and large dots. Early Corinthian. Late 7th cent.

Cf.: P a y n e, NC, p. 290, No. 564ff.; *CVA Schloss Fasanerie 2*, Pl. 60, 1; *CVA Gela 1*, Pl. 33, 1—6.

34. Aryballos Pl. XI

MNP A 22 (formerly Berlin, Antiquarium). Smyrna. H: 0.06, D: 0.057. Light clay with slightly pinkish shade. Brown lustrous glaze, in some places brick-red as a result of misfiring. Mouth glued together. Bibliography: *CVA Pologne 3*, Pl. 3/119/4 (and the references there cited); K u b c z a k, p. 163, Fig. 2; id., *Katalog*, No. 70.

Round aryballos with its body flattened, band handle running aslant and large, flat mouth. On the mouth four circles, on the rim dots. On the handle four horizontal stripes. On the shoulders tongues. On the body a broad band filled with dots (principally six rows), enclosed on both sides by three stripes. On the bottom three circles. Early — Middle Corinthian. Linear style.

Cf.: P a y n e, NC, p. 291, Fig. 127, No. 641; *CVA Heidelberg 1*, Pl. 12, 11; U r e, AFR, Pl. 5, 96—2. 145—2, p. 26—28 and *Appendix*, p. 92: IV. II. b; *CVA Gela 1*, Pl. 22, 4—6; L a u r e n s, p. 57, No. 13; *Corinth 15, 3*, p. 285, No. 1552, Pl. 63.

35. Pyxis Pl. XII

MNW 198007 (formerly Wrocław). H: 0.072 (with lid 0.12), D: 0.125. Yellowish clay. Black glaze (brownish-yellow in some places), partly worn off. Dark violet. Incisions. Bibliography: *CVA Pologne 5*, Pls. 16, 1—4 and 18, 5, Fig. 2; B e r n-h a r d, Fig. 51.

Cylindrical pyxis with concave walls having a lid. The walls of a pyxis and lid adorned with a band decoration (slanting zigzag, lines, dots in a chequered pattern, rays), in which the main zone is occupied by animal frieze: a panther opposit the buck, two panthers facing each other with a deer between them (on the lid another buck). In the background, abundant incised rosettes and dots. An identical frieze, regarding both the disposition and choice of animals, displaying also much stylistical similarity, is to be found on a pyxis lid from the Potters' Quarter in Corinth. Early Corinthian. 620—590.

Cf.: *Corinth 15, 3*, p. 86f., No. 390, Pl. 20; on shape P a y n e, NC, p. 292, Nos. 646ff.; H o p p e r, p. 205, also No. 15.

36. Skyphos   Pl. XIV

MNP A 63 (formerly Berlin, Antiquarium). Nola. H: 0.085, D: 0.115. Yellowish clay. Blackish-brown lustrous glaze. Purple for details. Incisions. Glued together. Bibliography: *CVA Pologne 3*, Pl. 3/119/2 (and the references there cited); K u b-c z a k, p. 168, Fig. 7a—c; id., *Katalog*, No. 74, Fig. 30.

Slender vase with a fairly narrow foot, walls flaring and in upper part inclined inwards and two horizontal handles just below the mouth. Interior glazed except for the band below the mouth. Between the handles vertical wavy bars. On the body, animal frieze: a panther opposite the goat, swan with raised wings (added paint on the abdomens, necks and wings). The animals' bodies are unproportionally elongated, while the legs remain short. Filling ornaments: rosettes and blobs. On the lower body rays. On the exterior and interior side of the foot glazed band. Workmanship neglectful. Early Corinthian. 620—590.

Cf.: similar are: *Corinth 7, 1*, Pl. 35, 256—259; *Corinth 7, 2*, Pls. 8—9; this type of decoration occurs also in Middle Corinthian, see Nos. 59—60.; on shape see Nos. 2 and 11.

37. Skyphos   Pl. XI

ZAŚ UJ 10.168. H: 0.004, D: 0.055. Light yellow clay. Black glaze with green shade. Glued together, mouth slightly jagged. Bibliography: *CVA Pologne 2*, Pl. 5/78/2; B e r n h a r d, *Katalog*, No. 313.

Small negligently made skyphos with a large, incision-separated foot and two large handles. Rim accentuated with a line. Between the handles groups of vertical wavy lines. On the body, frieze of three schematically painted dogs running to r., made in a silhouette technic, and enclosed within double lines. Foot painted from above. On the bottom circles. This vase represents the "running dog style", developing principally in Protocorinthian (cf. No. 8), which survived, however, down to Middle Corinthian. Early Corinthian. Late 7th — Early 6th cent.

Cf.: H o p p e r, p. 186; B r o c k, BSA 44, 1949, p. 51, No. 11, Pl. 18; H a y e s, *Tocra 1*, p. 21, Nos. 341—350, Pl. 25.

38. Amphora

Pl. XIV

MNW 198511 (1946, formerly Wrocław). H: 0.295, D: 0.24. Yellow clay with grey shade. Black, lustrous glaze, yellowish-orange in some places. Dark violet for details. Incisions. Small injuries, decoration worn in some places. Bibliography: *CVA Pologne 5*, Pls. 26, 1—4 and 28, 1—4 (and the references there cited).

Neck amphora with a conical foot, bulgy body narrow in its lower part, slightly convex shoulders, neck separated by two moulded rings, flaring mouth with a high rim and two handles. The mouth interior black except for a broader reserved band with two dark violet lines. Exterior part of the mouth, the neck and the handle black. On the shoulders siren and swan. On the body two friezes between stripes. Below rays. Foot glazed. Upper frieze: a panther oppostie the deer, lion opposite the panther, buck between those. Lower frieze: a bird with spread wings between the two lions, panther facing the ram. The animals are very alongated, on their necks, abdomens and hind quarters as well as on the necks and wings of the birds added paint. In the background incised rosettes, blobs, dots and elements resembling lotus flowers. Early Corinthian. 620—590.

Cf.: on shape P a y n e, NC, p. 300, Fig. 137, Nos. 769ff.; H o p p e r, p. 243f.; also No. 67.

39. Krater

Pl. XIII

MNW 142344 (Gołuchów coll.). H: 0.35, D: 0.435. Yellowish clay with green shade. Black lustrous glaze. Red and white applied. Incisions. Glued together, small part of body missing. Bibliography: *CVA Pologne 1*, Pl. 7, 1a—d (with the references there cited); H o p p e r, p. 168 and 250, 6; B e n s o n, GKV, p. 33, List 43, No. 1a (Art des Ebermalers); B e r n h a r d, Fig. 19; B a k i r, Beiträge zur Archäologie 7, 1974, p. 11, Grup II, No. K 12; A m y x, CorVP, p. 662 (cited for the hippocamps). See also: five stamps (1,50; 2; 4,20; 4,50 and 8 + 4 zł), Polish Mail 1976 (special issue for Postage Stamp Day, cf. also No. 24 above), siren, bull, lion, buck and sphinx.

Column-krater with horizontal handles reaching above the rim and connected with it by means of additional narrow piece of clay. On the upper surface of the rim animal frieze showing lions, panthers, goats, owls, sirens and a completely unique motif, hippocamps. On the shoulders in a metope a panther opposite the boar, swan between the two sirens. Below each handle seated sphinx to l. The body decorated by animal frieze: a siren with spread wings to r. between the boar and buck, boar to r. between the bull and panther to r. between the bull and buck. The animals in all friezes are painted very skilfully; the bulls attract attention apart from the mentioned hippocamps. Added paint occurs on the necks, abdomens and hind quarters of the animals, on the bucks' horns, faces and necks of the sirens and on wings and tails of the birds. On the swan's neck on the mouth frieze three large dots. In the friezes' background (yet not below the handles), dense filling ornament: incised rosettes, rosette-flowers with small double circles in the centre, spots and dots. The main frieze enclosed from above by a narrow, from below by a wide black band (both with added red stripes and white lines). On the lower body rays. Foot black with two red stripes enclosed by white ones. Handles and pieces of clay linking them to the mouth, neck and rim black. According to J. L. Benson this vase represents "Manner of" his Boar Painter (GKV, p. 33, List 43: Eber Maler), but Prof. Amyx does not agree with this opinion: "Benson's «Ebermaler» is not a valiable concept; still less, «Manner of...»" (private letter, August 26, 1987). Early Corinthian. 600—590.

Cf.: on shape P a y n e, NC, p. 300—302, Nos. 776—781A; H o p p e r, p. 249f; B a k i r, Beiträge zur Archäologie 7, passim; C a l l i p o l i t i s - F e y t m a n s, BCH 101, 1977, p. 235—239; similar panther and boar on aryballos *CVA Louvre* 8, Pl. 17, 3, 6—7, 9—10; animal frieze on top of rim is very unusual, but cf. Louvre E 635 (Eurytios krater), P o t t i e r, *Vases ant. du Louvre*, 1, p. 56ff. (I owe this quotation to Prof. Amyx).

2.5. MIDDLE CORINTHIAN

40. Alabastron   Pl. XV

MNP A 742 (Gołuchów coll.). H: 0.225, D: 0.125. Yellowish clay. Black glaze. Red applied. Incisions. Mouth slightly jagged, decoration worn off in some places. Bibliography: *CVA Pologne 1*, Pl. 6, 10 (and the references there cited); H o p p e r, p. 193, 7; B e n s o n, GKV, p. 118, No. 395.

Large alabastron with a very narrow neck. On the mouth around the orifice circles and tongues; similar pattern on the bottom. On the rim small dots between two lines. On the neck elongated tongues. The handle decorated with a black stripe. The body adorned by a large floral ornament comprising four lotus flowers crosswise, linked by a black circle with an incised rosette inside. Between the lotus flowers, two buds at the top and two leaves at the base. On the lotus flowers the series are visible of delicate white dots between the two incised lines. On the back, swan to r. In the background dense filling ornament. The body's decoration is enclosed on both sides by double lines. Middle Corinthian. Early phase. White-dot-style.

Cf.: P a y n e, NC, p. 303, group C and n. 3, p. 285, Nos. 433—439 and p. 146f., Fig. 53—54 (on motif of four lotus flowers); similar decoration in white-dot-style: *CVA Louvre 8*, Pl. 17, 1, 2, 4, 5; CVA Frankfurt a/M 1, Pl. 14, 4—6 (= P a y n e, NC, No. 436); Lo Porto, p. 105, complesso 51, Figs. 82a and 83; Cl. Rh. 3, Jalyssos gr. 45, 16, p. 78, Pl. VI (white-dot-style?); similar floral composition also on aryballoi Nos. 43 and 44.

41. Aryballos   Pl. XI

MNW 199243. H: 0.044, D: 0.057. Yellow clay. Black, lustrous glaze, brown in some places. Incisions. Missing: fragment of mouth. Decoration almost entirely worn off. Bibliography: *CVA Pologne 5*, Pls. 33, 1 and 10, 3.

Round aryballos with a slightly flattened body and broad mouth with a flaring rim. On the mouth tongues between circles. On the handle traces of horizontal bars. At the neck's base tongues. On the body standing sphinx of massive proportions and alongated body to r., which is painted very clumsy. Near the sphinx two small rosettes. On the bottom concentric circles. Middle Corinthian. 590—570.

Cf.: P a y n e cites two only examples of standing sphinxes: NC, p. 89, No. 862 and p. 315; on the sphinx generally V e r d e l i s, BCH 85, 1951, p. 1ff.; CVA Mainz 1, Pl. 29, 1—3.

42. Aryballos   Pl. XI

ZAŚ UJ 10.166 (donated by W. Czartoryski, 1872). H: 0.055, D: 0.06. Yellow clay. Blackish-brown glaze (traces only). Incisions. Decoration almost entirely worn off. Bibliography: CVA Pologne 2, Pl. 4/77/17; B e r n h a r d, Katalog, No. 315; P a p u c i - W ł a d y k a, No. 6.

Round vase, somewhat flattened, with a large, flaring up mouth, which is concave on both sides. On the rim a series of small dots. Handle edges glazed. On the body traces of the representation of a siren (?) with spread wings. On the bottom whirling bows between two circles. The Cracow object corresponds with a group D of Early Corinthian aryballoi in Payne's classification. However, the shape and proportions of the mouth, which according to Benson are characteristic for the Middle Corinthian, allow us to date No. 42 at this period. Midde Corinthian. 590—570.

Cf.: P a y n e, NC, p. 289, Fig. 125 (Lion Group); B e n s o n, AJA 68, 1964, p. 169.

43. Aryballos   Pl. XI

MNW 198029 (formerly Wrocław). H: 0.068, D: 0.074. Light yellow clay with green shade. Black glaze, brown in some places, partly worn off. Red added. Incisions. Bibliography: CVA Pologne 5, Pls. 34, 1—3 and 36, 6.

Round aryballos with a strongly flattened body and massive mouth. On the mouth tongues between double circles; on its rim vertical zig-zags. On the handle between its glazed edges three horizontal bars. On the body, four lotus flowers crosswise; between the flowers and behind them rosettes resembling the "whirling" type and blobs (some incised). Above and below three lines. On the bottom concentric circles. Comparing to the careful and very much elaborated version of the four lotus flowers motif, observed on the alabastron No. 39, the same motif in the case of the discussed aryballos is treated in a simplified and clumsy way, which indicates — as well as the whirling rosettes (on those see Nos. 54, 56) — on the later phase of Middle Corinthian.

44. Arybalos

Pl. XI

ZAŚ UJ 10.165 (donated by W. Czartoryski). H: 0.065, D: 0.07. Yellow clay. Black, semi-lustrous glaze (partly brick-red as a result of misfiring). Red applied. Incisions. Mouth slightly jagged, decoration partly worn off. Bibliography: *CVA Pologne 2*, Pl. 4/77/16; B e r n h a r d, *Katalog*, No. 317; P a p u c i - W ł a d y k a, No. 13.

Round aryballos with a slightly flattened body and large mouth with its upper surface and rim concave. On the mouth tongues enclosed within circles; on the rim tiny dots. On the shoulders short tongues. On the bottom five circles of various width. On the body a small palmette and three lotus flowers crosswice, between those two leaves and two buds. Middle Corinthian. 590—570. Payne's "Lion Group: florals" (Amyx).

Cf.: P a y n e, NC, p. 289, No. 553f.; A m y x, CorVP, pp. 124ff.; similar shape and decoration's arrangement.

45. Arybalos

Pl. XVI

MDP (without inventory No.). H: 0.063, D: 0.069. Light yellow clay. Black, mat glaze. Incisions. Decoration heavily worn off. Bibliography: G r a b o w s k i, *Muzeum Diecezjalne w Płocku*, p. 84 (mentioned only).

Round aryballos with a distorted mouth with a concave bottom, pointing downwards. On the mouth concentric circles, on the rim large dots. On the handle three horizontal stripes. On the shoulders tongues, below two lines. On the frontal body four warriors (helmets, shields, spears) to l. On the shields' edges white dots, and in their centres three slanting incised lines (central wavy). No filling ornament. The described vase has the traits of the warrior aryballoi of group b in Ures' classification. Middle Corinthian. 590—580.

Cf.: U r e, AFR, p. 23 and 38—39, IV.VI.b; see also No. 28; most similar are: *CVA Gela 1*, Pl. 42, 1—5; L o P o r t o, p. 116, complesso 57, 2, Fig. 91b. List of warrior aryballoi: U r e, AFR, p. 97—99, *Appendix* IV.VI; add M a f f r e, BCH 95, 1971, p. 630 n. 20 (and p. 629 n. 10—13, concerning this motif on other vases' types); *CVA Gela 1*, Pls. 26—27.

46. Arybalos

Pl. XVI

MNW 198031 (1946, formerly Wrocław). H: 0.054, D: 0.055. Yellow clay. Black, semi-lustrous glaze. Red added. Incisions. Missing: fragment of mouth. Surface worn. Bibliography: *CVA Pologne 5*, Pl. 36, 7—9.

On the body three warriors marching to r. (eyes and hair marked) with spears poised forwards. The shields' inner fields separated with incised circles, bear added paint and are cut by three slanting incised lines. Between the warriors series of dots painted around the upper sections of spears and between the shields. Other decorative elements similar to the aryballos No. 45. Classification and dating as No. 45.

Cf.: *CVA Louvre 6*, Pl. 6, 3 — identical style.

47. Aryballos

Pl. XVI

ZAŚ UJ 10.164 (Chlebowski coll., 1925). H: 0.06, D: 0.06. Buff clay. Black, semi-lustrous glaze. Red applied. Incisions. Glued together, partly damaged, decoration worn off in several places. Bibliography: *CVA Pologne 2*, Pl. 4/77/15; B e r n h a r d, *Katalog*, No. 316; P a p u c i - W ł a d y k a, No. 8.

Round aryballos. On the mouth and its rim circles. On the shoulders tongues. On the frontal body four warriors to r. (helmets and eyes marked). Inner field of the shields with added red; on the shields-edges white dots. In the background dot rosettes. Classification and dating as No. 45.

48. Aryballos

Pl. XVI

MNW 23825 (donated by K. Firich). H: 0.064, D: 0.063. Yellowish clay with slightly red shade. Blackish-brown glaze, heavily worn off. Red for details. Incisions. Bibliography: *CVA Pologne 3*, Pl. 1/104/13.

Round aryballos with a slightly flattened body and large mouth of a somewhat concave surface. On the mouth and handle bands. On the body a frieze of three warriors with shields, marching to r. (prominent noses, beards, marked hair and ears). Central parts of the shields with added paints. In the background shaded rosettes. Above the frieze three lines, below circle occupying the bottom. Middle Corinthian. 580—570.

Cf.: No. 45; *CVA Karlsruhe 1*, Pl. 42, 3; concerning shaded rosettes which are typical for late phase of Middle Corinthian see No. 67.

49. Aryballos

Pl. XVI

MNW 198028 (1946, formerly Wrocław). H: 0.059, D: 0.061. Dark yellow clay. Black, semi-lustrous glaze, in several places worn off. Incisions. Bibliography: *CVA Pologne 5*, Pl. 36, 4—5.

Round aryballos with a distorted body. Mouth, shoulders and bottom as in case of No. 45. On the handle with glazed edges, three horizontal bars. On the body a frieze of four warriors marching to r. with helmets and spears. The middle parts of the shields distinguished by incised lines, but without added paints. No filling ornament. Very clumsy workmanship. The Warsaw object corresponds with the aryballoi of group c in Ures' classification. End of the Middle Corinthian. Ca 570.

Cf.: U r e, AFR, p. 23, 39, IV.VI.c; *CVA Reading 1*, Pl. 4, 7—11, p. 8—9 (Ure); *CVA Heidelberg 1*, Pl. 12, 12; *CVA Tübingen 1*, Pl. 26, 3; *CVA Mainz, Zentralmuseum 1*, Pl. 17, 9.

50. Aryballos

Pl. XVII

MNW 198536 (formerly Wrocław). H: 0.115, D: 0.107. Yellowish clay. Black, lustrous glaze. Traces of red applied. Incisions. Bibliography: *CVA Pologne 5*, Pl. 32, 1—5 (and the references there cited); M i c h a ł o w s k i, *Sztuka starożytna*, Fig. 50; B e r n h a r d, Fig. 168; B e n s o n, AntK 14, 1971, p. 14 sub No. 12; A m y x, CorVP, p. 180, No. c-1.

Broad-bottomed aryballos with a low foot. On the mouth circles, on the rim stripe. On the flat handle zigzag. On the shoulders, tongues. The body with a figural scene: bearded squat man (hair-band, robe sinking down the shoulders, spear in his right hand, winged boots on the legs) — Hermes? — hastening to r., shown between two sirens. In the background incised and whirling rosettes. The scene is bordered from above by three, and from below by two lines. On the bottom, circles. End of Middle Corinthian. Related to the Otterlo Painter (Benson, Amyx).

Cf.: P a y n e, NC, p. 305, Nos. 835A—840; Hermes between panthers D u g a s, EAD 10, Pl. 26, No. 357 (= P a y n e, NC, No. 828) — Master of Animals according to C h i t t e n d e r, Hesperia 16, 1947, p. 89—114, esp. 104f., Pl. 18 C; on Otterlo Painter: B e n s o n, op. cit., p. 13ff.; A m y x, CorVP, loc. cit.

51. Ring aryballos   Pl. XV

MNW 198035 (1946, formerly Wrocław). H: 0.068, D: 0.058. Yellow clay. Blackish-brown, mat glaze (brownish-yellow in some places). Red (very altered) for details. Incisions. Surface worn off. Mouth slightly jagged. Bibliography: *CVA Pologne 5*, Pl. 29, 5—7 and Fig. 4.

On the mouth, tongues between the circles. On the rim, short tongues and a stripe. On the shoulders, tongues. On the ring, a rider on a horse of an extremely elongated shape, going to l., behind him another similar horse without a rider. In the background, spots assuming the shape of the free space, out by oblique incised lines. On each side of the ring: black band with radially distributed incised lines. Workmanship not very careful, Middle — Late Corinthian. 590—550.

Cf.: U r e, Hesperia 15, 1946, p. 38ff. (group B); *CVA Heidelberg 1*, Pl. 19, 2; also P a y n e, NC, p. 313, No. 1057ff.; H o p p e r, p. 248f.; *Corinth 15,3*, p. 159, No. 815, Pl. 37.

52. Pyxis   Pl. XVIII

MNW 142440 (Gołuchów coll.). H: 0.055, D: 0.10. Yellow clay. Blackish-brown, mat glaze. Mouth slightly jagged. Bibliography: *CVA Pologne 1*, Pl. 6, 3 (and the references there cited); H o p p e r, p. 191, 3.

Cylindrical pyxis with concave sides and two horizontal handles. Inside: bands and stripes. On the bottom circles surrounding a dot. Below the rim, a series of dots in a chequered pattern between three lines. On the body, a primitive frieze in a silhouette technic, showing four horses (?) and a dog. In the background: zigzag, glaze stains, chevrons, rosettes resembling the dotted type. Below: rays. This vase represents the so-called silhouette style, developing beside the orientalizing pottery mainstream, or, strictly speaking, one of its derivations defined as the "straggling type" (we have already become familiar with another offshoot — the "running dog style", cf. Nos. 8 and 37), which had been appearing since Early to the end of Middle Corinthian. Rosettes similar to dotted type appear only in the later phase of Middle Corinthian (cf. P a y n e, NC, p. 157, Fig. 69 B). A similar decoration occurs on a pyxis from Oxford. Middle Corinthian? Silhouette style.

Cf.: on "straggling type" H o p p e r, p. 190—191; *CVA Oxford 2*, Pl. 1, 55 and 3, 10; H a y e s, *Tocra 1*, p. 31, No. 160, Pl. 13 (animals silhouette style, no filling ornaments).

53. Pyxis
Pl. XIX

ZAŚ UJ 10.178 (donated by W. Czartoryski). H: 0.10, D: 0.125. Light yellow clay with red shade. Brown glaze, partly brick-red. Red for details. Incisions. Mouth slightly jagged, decoration partly worn off. Bibliography: *CVA Pologne 2*, Pl. 5/78/4; B e r n h a r d, *Katalog*, No. 311; P a p u c i, RechA Crac 1977, p. 62, No. 3, Fig. 1: A.

Convex-sided pyxis without handles on a conical, low foot. On the body a frieze showing a deer between the panthers, and a boar. In the background, incised rosettes, glaze stains and dots. The frieze is enclosed from above by two and from below by one reserved bands, filled with dots in a chequered pattern between lines. Middle Corinthian. 590—570.

Cf.: on shape C a l l i p o l i t i s - F e y t m a n s, AE 1973, p. 1—18, Pls. 1—3; similar in shape are *CVA Heidelberg 1*, Pl. 17, 4; *Corinth 13, 1*, p. 181, gr. 156—11, p. 185. gr. 157-v, Pl. 23.

54. Pyxis
Pl. XX and XXI

MC A 1/1 (bought in 1845, according to inventory note "found in a sarcophagus in Acropolis at Athens"?) H: 0.130, with lid 0.170, D: 0.102 (rim), 0.183 (body). Light yellow clay. Blackish-brown glaze, red in some places. Red for details. Incisions. Several fragments of lid are missing, the rest is glued together. Decoration partly worn off; coarse crust in several places. Bibliography: unpublished.

Pyxis with convex walls, two handles attached at the shoulders, which points aslant upwards and a convex lid, having a high rim with a hooped lug of a circular cross-section. On the lid: two bands with groups of vertical zigzags, one with dot rosettes. Decoration of pyxis: rim red inside and black outside, two lines, on the shoulders double palmette chain, below three stripes (lateral red), animal frieze, black line, groups of vertical zigzags, double line of dots in a chequered pattern, rays. Foot: red. On the bottom circles of glaze and red paint. The frieze represents nine figures: a bird with its head turned back between a seated griffon and sphinx; a griffon-bird to r., a siren with her head turned back, two seated sphinxes facing each other (that on the r. in a polos), between them a swan to r., next siren to r. and another siren also to r., yet with a head turned back. Rich added colours on necks, wings and hind quarters of the animals. In the background, incised rosettes, as well as whirling and resembling the star-rosettes, and a few dots. The filling ornaments and the vase's shape point to late phase of Middle Corinthian. Identical ornaments, particularly the whirling rosettes occur on an oinochoe from Munich (former Schoen coll.). Middle Corinthian. Late phase.

Cf.: L u l l i e s, *Eine Sammlung griechische Kleinkunst,* p. 22, Pl. 15, No. 43; P a y n e, NC, p. 307, No. 895 (on ahape), p. 157, Figs. 68, 69 (on filling ornament), p. 156 (on double palmette chain).

55. Pyxis
Pl. XVI

MC A 2/2. H: 0.09, D: 0.115, Light yellow clay. Brown glaze (traces only). Glued together. Surface partly "corroded". Bibliography: unpublished.

Shape similar to No. 54, lid lacking. On the shoulders: three stripes. On the handle vertical bars, handle-ridges glazed. Below, three bands of a dotted ornament in a chequered pattern between the lines. Foot glazed (?). On the bottom: traces of circles. Middle Corinthian. 590—570.

Cf.: *CVA Heidelberg 1,* Pl. 17, 11 (identical shape, similar decoration); *Corinth 13,1,* Pl. 23, 157-p (but more spherical body and zigzags in handle-band).

56. Pyxis
Pl. XXI

MNW 198513 (formerly Wrocław). H: 0.17, D: 0.198. Yellowish clay. Black glaze, brownish-yellow in some places. Red for details. Incisions. Lid glued together. On lower body and foot calcareous (?) crust. Bibliography: *CVA Pologne 5,* Pls. 17, 1—6 and 18, 1—2; B e r n h a r d, Fig. 50; A m y x, CSCA 4, 1971, p. 34, List 9, No. 2; A m y x, CorVP, p. 217, No. B-3.

Type as No. 54, yet the body more globular, whereas the lid with a flat, button-shaped lug. The lid: concentric circles (some red). Pyxis: mouth black (also inside), below a red stripe, two friezes parted by four stripes (those marginal red), still below three stripes (the outer ones red). Upper frieze: on both sides of the vase a buck opposite the panther; below the handles, a bird with its head turned back. Lower frieze: swan between the panthers, a panther to r. between the bucks going to l. Incisions fairly careful. Parts of the animals' bodies and birds' wings with added red. The filling ornaments: incised rosettes, glaze spots, whirling rosettes and dots. End of Middle Corinthian — beginning of Late Corinthian. Near the Geladakis Painter (Amyx).

Cf.: on shape No. 54; P a y n e, NC, p. 307, Fig. 142; H o p p e r, p. 211; D u n b a b i n, *Perachora 2,* p. 174; on Geladakis Painter A m y x, CSCA 4, 1971, p. 29—41; *Corinth 13,1,* p. 179, gr. 155-a, Pls. A and 85, p. 99; *Corinth 7,2,* p. 106, An 36, Pls. 57, 96; B e n s o n, AJA 85, 1981, p. 173, No. 16.

57. Pyxis
Pl. XVIII

MNW 142439 (Gołuchów coll.). H: 0.075, D: 0.05. Buff clay with green shade. Black, lustrous glaze. Bibliography: *CVA Pologne 1,* Pl. 6, 4 (and the references there cited); H o p p e r, p. 189, 216, 5.

Tripod-pyxis with a thickened mouth and conical lid with a knobby lug. Decoration in silhouette technic. The vase's legs are adorned with representations in metopes: on two, seated sphinxes to r., on the 3rd, a seated panther. On the upper body, a stripe. The mouth black on both sides. On the inside: a circle. The lid: on the edge, dots, above an animal frieze with two sphinxes, a panther and a swan. In the background, spots of various shapes and dots along the animals' tails. Middle — Late Corinthian. Silhouette style.

Cf.: for shape, subject and technic pyxis from Corinth: *Corinth 13, 1*, p. 116, 143, and p. 212, gr. 253—3, Pl. 35 (= A m y x, CorVP, p. 427, 455 n. 52); finer than our, and it has a near twin in Argos Museum (I owe this reference to Prof. Amyx); *CVA Hoppin Coll.*, Pl. 1, 3 (similar shape).

58. Pyxis lid Pl. XXII

MNW 147979 (1951, formerly Archaeological Museum in Warsaw). H: 0.059, D: 0.17. Light yellow clay. Black, semi-lustrous glaze. Incisions. Glued together, partly restored, decoration worn off in some places. Bibliography: *CVA Pologne 5*, Pl. 18, 3. 4. 6. and Fig. 3.

A slightly convex lid with a mushroom-shaped lug, at its base provided with a plastic ring. On the lug, tongues (three black, one reserved) surrounded with a black line. Similar tongues (only black) on the lid, then two lines and an animal frieze: a group of two sirens, between them the 3rd siren going to r. with her head turned back; a panther turns on this group from the r., and a buck from the l. The remaining part of the frieze is taken by partially preserved quadrupeds facing each other: a panther (or lion) and a buck (or deer). Dense filling ornament: incised rosettes, small blobs and abundant tiny dots. At the lid's edge, a double series of dots between the lines, three stripes and three incised grooves. The decoration, and especially the filling ornament resembles the Middle Corinthian "delicate style". Middle Corinthian. 590—570.

Cf.: on lids of pyxides D u n b a b i n, *Perachora 2*, p. 175; H o p p e r, p. 208; on "delicate style" e.g. P a y n e, NC, Pl. 28, 11; A m y x, CorV, Pls. 28, 29a—c.

59. Skyphos Pl. XIV

MNW 198021 (1946, formerly Wrocław). H: 0.129, D: 0.253. Light yellow clay. Black lustrous glaze, partly worn off. Red applied. Surface damaged, mouth slightly jagged, one handle glued together. Bibliography: *CVA Pologne 5*, Pl. 22, 1—4; B e r n h a r d, Fig. 167.

Broad-based skyphos with a conical foot and the walls slightly inverted in the upper part. Interior glazed. Between the handles, densely distributed wavy lines. On the body, a frieze shows unproportionally elongated animals: a buck to r. between two panthers and a bird to r. with its head turned back. Added paints and filling ornaments traditional. On the lower body rays. Foot black. On the bottom, circles. Middle Corinthian. 590—570.

Cf.: P a y n e, NC, p. 308, No. 928ff.; B e n s o n, Hesperia 52, 1983, p. 321ff.; *Corinth 15, 3*, p. 117f., Nos. 575—576, Pl. 27.

60. Skyphos   Pl. XIV

MNW 198004 (1946, formerly Wrocław). H: 0.107, D: 0.227. Whitish clay. Blackish-brown glaze, red on half of vase. Red for details. Incisions. Decoration partly worn off. Bibliography: *CVA Pologne 5*, Pls. 24, 25; B e n s o n, Hesperia 52, 1983, p. 321.

Shape as a former, a base broader. The decoration also very nearing, yet the rays more densely distributed, on the foot one red and two black bands; in a frieze: two bucks to r. with a bird between them and a panther to l. Middle Corinthian. Near the Painter of KP 64 (Benson).

Cf.: No. 59; B e n s o n, op. cit. (bibliography of the item).

61. Skyphos   Pl. XXII

MC A 5/5 (donatetd by Kniczek from Místek, 1846). H: 0.042, D: 0.065, with handles 0.102. Yellow clay. Blackish-brown glaze. Red applied. Whitish crust in some places. Bibliography: unpublished.

Small broad-based skyphos with a massive foot and almost straight walls. Interior glazed except for the rim. Handles glazed. On the rim: a line. In the handle band ornament of elements resembling the reversed "z". On the body, two rows of short vertical lines, parted by a black line bordered by two broad red bands and black lines. Foot black, also on the bottom. On the bottom of skyphos: circles. Middle — Late Corinthian. 1st half of 6th cent. Linear style.

Cf.: *CVA Wien, Universität 1*, Pl. 4, 10 (similar shape); similar ornament in main band: *Corinth 13, 1*, p. 172, gr. 135—1, Pl. 18, p. 101 n. 26; K o k k o u- -V i r i d i, AE 1980, p. 46, No. 58, Pl. 24; see also Nos. 90—91.

62. Cup   Pl. XIV

MC A 7/7. H: 0.065, D: 0.145, with handles 0.188. Light yellow clay. Blackish- -brown glaze (traces only). Incisions. Dark coloured crust on great part of vase. Bibliography: unpublished.

Deep cup on a short conical foot with a strongly offset rim. Inside, on the rim and on the handles: traces of glaze. On the body, traces of a frieze preserved: on one side a griffon-bird and a water bird (swan?) to r., on the other, a griffon-bird to l. The frieze bordered on both sides by three lines. Middle Corinthian. 590—570.

Cf.: P a y n e, NC, p. 310f., Fig. 152, Nos. 977ff.; H o p p e r, p. 225f; see also No. 83.

63. Oinochoe Pls. XVI and XIX

MNW 198022 (formerly Wrocław). H: 0.188, D: 0.173. Buff clay with green shade. Blackish-brown, lustrous glaze. Red for details. Incisions. Decoration almost entirely worn off. Bibliography: *CVA Pologne 5*, Pls. 19—20 and 21, 1—2.

Broad-bottomed oinochoe with a high, cylindrical neck with moulded ring. Lid, mouth, neck, and handle were glazed. On the shoulders a bar ornament. Below: a broad red-margined black band, a double series of dots between the lines. On the upper body, an animal frieze: in the middle an ornament of the palmette and lotus flower, flanked by two griffon-birds and a panther on the l. and a lion on the r. Below the handle, a panther to l. between the buck and boar. The animals are heavily proportioned and of elongated silhouettes. Traces of added paints on their necks, abdomens and wings. Dense filling ornament. Below the frieze, a broad black band, a line, rays. Glazed annular base. Middle Corinthian. 590—570.

Cf.: on shape P a y n e, NC, p. 277, 299, 315, 325; H o p p e r, p. 237—238; Nos. 64—65 are another variety of this shape.

64. Oinochoe Pl. XXIII

MNP A 448. H: 0.145, D: 0.103. Light yellowish clay. Brown glaze. Red for details. Incisions. Missing: part of body. Glued together, decoration worn off. Bibliography: K u b c z a k, p. 107f., Figs. 9, 10; id., *Katalog*, p. 48, No. 77.

Broad-bottomed oinochoe of a shape nearing to the former, yet with a short, broad neck lacking the moulded ring. Mouth, neck handle and shoulders as in No. 63. On the body, animal frieze bordered by bands (some of them with red added), showing the group of a deer to r. (preserved in fragments), between two panthers; below the handle, a bird to r. (eagle, dove?). Filling ornament: incised rosettes, whirling and shaded rosettes and blobs, characteristic of the final stage of Middle Corinthian. End of Middle Corinthian. Saint-Raymond Painter (Amyx).

Cf.: A m y x, CorVP, p. 223, Pl. 91, 3—4 and p. 322, 349 with reference to L u k e s h, AJA 84, 1980, p. 184ff., Pls. 30—31.

65. Oinochoe Pl. XXIV

MNP A 21 (formerly Antiquarium, Berlin). Nola. H: 0.12, D: 0.10. Light yellowish clay. Brown glaze (red on half of body). Added red and white paint. Missing: fragment of mouth. Bibliography: *CVA Pologne 3*, Pl. 3/119/3 (and the references there cited); K u b c z a k, p. 169, Fig. 8; id. *Katalog*, No. 75.

Shape as No. 64. The whole vase glazed. Its neck distinguished by two white lines. On the shoulders: a bar ornament of red and glazed elements alternately. On the shoulders-into-body transition and on the lowest body, a purple stripe enclosed within two white ones. The decoration of the described object belongs to the so-called "black polychrome" type (cf. Nos. 9, 10), known earlier and used also in the 6th cent. Middle Corinthian. 590—570.

Cf.: No. 64 (on shape); *Corinth 13, 1*, p. 181, gr. 156—6, Pl. 20.

66. Exaleiptron   Pl. XXIV

MNW 142444 (Gołuchów coll.). H: 0.065, D: 0.215. Dark yellow clay with orange shade. Black, lustrous glaze with olive shade. Bibliography: *CVA Pologne 1*, Pl. 6, 8 (and the references there cited); H o p p e r, p. 232, 4; A m y x, CorVP, p. 352, No. A-3.

Exaleiptron with an omega-shaped handle. Interior glazed except for the central portion with two circles. Around the orifice an animal frieze: opposite the handle the group of a siren to r. with reposed wings and a head turned back between the similar sirens, yet having sickle- -shaped wings; on both sides of this group, a panther facing it. Next on the l., a bull (?) opposite the bird, on the r., a panther opposite the buck. This animals are painted rather clumsily. Incisions are rich, but careless and dashing — the lines frequently transgress the figures' area. Filling ornaments are lacking. The frieze is enclosed by a glazed line and a double series of dots between the lines. Foot red. On the bottom, red and black circles. Handle black. An identically shaped and similarly decorated is the exaleiptron from Brussels, adorned with representations of goat and panthers in a style identical to the Warsaw object. Such a specific style is to be encountered also on the exaleiptra from Kassel and Louvre. This unusual likeness of shape, similar arrangement of decoration and the convergence of the paintings' stylistic traits on all the four objects, enable their recognition as the works of the same artist, whom I dare to propose to be named Painter of Gołuchów Exaleiptron. Prof. Amyx calls the artist "Fiesole Painter" and attributes him also the vase from Fiesole, Coll. Constantini. The dating of the painter's activity may be determined to the last years of Middle and the first years of Late Corinthian. Painter of Gołuchów Exaleiptron (= Professor's Amyx Fiesole Painter).

Cf.: *CVA Bruxelles 3*, Pl. 7a—b; *CVA Kassel 2*, Pl. 50, 1—3 (= P a y n e, NC, p. 314. No. 1089 A); P o t t i e r, *Les vases antiques du Louvre*, p. 50, No. E 551, Pl. 42; detailed study concerning the Painter of Gołuchów Exaleiptron is being prepared by the author of the present work. Concerning the name of this type of vases (otherwise "kothons") see: S c h e i b l e r, JdI 79, 1964, p. 72ff.; ead., AA 1968, p. 389ff.; this shape appears for the first time in Transitional Period (see A n d e r s o n, BSA 53—54, 1958—59, p. 143, No. 78, Pl. 23 — fragment from Old Smyrna), but very popular become after 550, see Nos. 92—99. For general lite- rature see: B u r r o w s - U r e, JHS 31, 1911, p. 72ff.; Σίνδος. Κατάλογος τῆς ἐκθέσης Nos. 403, 412.

67. Amphora   Pl. XXV

ZAŚ UJ 10.215 (donated by W. Czartoryski, 1872), H: 0.195, D: 0.15. Light yellow clay. Blackish-brown glaze. Red for details. Incisions. Glued together.

Bibliography: *CVA Pologne 2*, Pl. 5/78/5; H o p p e r, p. 243, 2; B e r n h a r d, *Katalog*, No. 310.

Neck amphora with a conical foot; aquat body, flat shoulders, slightly flaring neck ending in somewhat concave mouth and two band handles. On the handles, horizontal bars. A vertical stripe runs through the middle of the neck, on its both sides. At the neck's base: a black stripe. On the shoulders, a bar ornament. Below: two stripes, a frieze enclosed within a broad band bordered with red stripes, rays. Foot black. In the frieze six animals: a lion to r. opposite the panther turning its head back (snout en face), a bull going to r. facing the ram (?), a grazing deer to r. and a bird with reposed wings going in the same direction. The animals are painted both clumsily and negligently. Incisions hurried and slapdash. In the background, shaded rosettes of a very irregular form, rosettes with a circle in centre, numerous dots. The described vase represents rather mediocre style. The nearest to the Cracow amphora with regard to the shape and the disposition of decoration is an amphora from Gela, bearing also shaded rosettes. Middle Corinthian. Late phase. 580—570.

Cf.: No. 38 (on shape); *CVA Gela 2*, Pl. 18; on shaded rosettes: P a y n e, NC, p. 322, No. 1306, Pl. 28, 7; D u n b a b i n, *Perachora 2*, p. 258, No. 2510, Pl. 104; *Corinth 13, 1*, p. 180, gr. 115-c, Pl. 22, 88; *CVA Bucarest 2*, Pl. 4, 3—6.

2.6. LATE CORINTHIAN I

68. Alabastron   Pl. XXVI

MNW 198024 (formerly in Silesia). H: 0.09, D: 0.038. Yellow but discoloured, soft clay. Blackish-brown glaze. Incisions. Decoration heavily worn off. Bibliography: *CVA Pologne 5*, Pls. 29, 1—4 and 30, 1.

Small slender alabastron with relatively broad neck and massive mouth. On the mouth, short tongues between the circles. On the rim elongated dots. On the neck: tongues. The whole body is occupied by the picture of a large cock with spread wings to r. In the background several rosettes. The representations is enclosed on both sides by three stripes. On the bottom, tongues around the circle. Not very careful workmanship. Late Corinthian. 570—550.

Cf.: P a y n e, NC, p. 319, Nos. 1200ff., group A of small alabastra.

69. Aryballos   Pl. XXVI

MNW 31793 (J. Choynowski coll.). From Berezan Isle. H: 0.071, D: 0.075. Buff clay with green shade. Blackish-brown glaze (brownish-yellow in some places). Dark violet on foils. Decoration worn off in some places. Bibliography: *CVA Pologne 3*, Pl. 1/106/9 (and the reference there cited).

Round aryballos with a flattened body and large mouth with a high rim. On the body, a large quatrefoil motif situated on the vessel's axis, composed of symmetrically disposed four petals, surrounded by a line. Between the foils, on the body's each side, a cross-hatched leaf of a shape nearing to the hexagon; these leaves are linked by means of an oval circumlining the vertical line. From below, the petals are connected by three horizontal bars (between the second and the third, a horizontal zigzag); to the lowest the tongues adjoin, which are framed by glaze lines. Between the upper petals: comb pattern. The described aryballos belongs to a large group of the "quatrefoil" aryballoi, which started to occur already in Early Corinthian, but had mainly been fluorishing in the years 580—550. After the middle of the 6th cent. they happen to appear more rarely. Middle — Late Corinthian I. 580—550.

Cf.: P a y n e, NC, p. 146—148, Fig. 54, p. 320f., No. 1263, Fig. 161, group F; U r e, AFR, p. 43—45, 101—103; *CVA Reading 1*, Pl. 1—4; H o p p e r, p. 201; L o P o r t o, p. 97f.; *Corinth 13, 1*, p. 114; H a y e s, *Tocra 1*, p. 30; *CVA Gela 1*, Pls. 37—39; L a u r e n s, p. 85f., No. 31; *CVA Tübingen 1*, Pl. 27, 1—2; G j e r s t a d, *Greek Pottery*, Pls. 27, 7—8 and 28, 4—7.

70. Aryballos   Pl. XXVII

MNK XI-A-353 (purchased from W. Terlecki, 1908). H: 0.067, D: 0.063. Buff clay. Brown glaze. Balow a handle a small part is glued together. Decoration havily worn off. Bibliography: *CVA Pologne 2*, Pl. 1/96/2; P a p u c i - W ł a d y k a, No. 11.

An aryballos simiar to the former, yet with large dots on its shoulders. Classification and dating as No. 69.

71. Aryballos   Pl. XXVII

MNK XI-A-354 (donated by A. Sulkiewicz, 1913). Panticapaion. H: 0.039, D: 0.04. Buff clay. Blackish-brown glaze. Decoration heavily worn off. Bibliography: P a p u c i - W ł a d y k a, No. 10.

Very small aryballos with a decoration as No. 69. Classification and dating as No. 69.

72. Aryballos   Pl. XXVI

MNW 198937 (formerly Ząbkowice, now deposit in the University of Wrocław). H: 0.067, D: 0.065. Yellowish clay. Blackish-brown glaze. Glued together. Bibliography: *CVA Pologne 5*, Pl. 35, 1—3.

Quatrefoil aryballos. On the mouth, one wide and two narrower circles. The handle adorned with a horizontal bar, running halfway its height. Other decorative elements as No. 69. Classification and dating as No. 69.

73. Aryballos   Pl. XXVI

MNW 198026 (formerly in Silesia). H: 0.068, D: 0.062. Yellow clay. Black glaze, brownish-yellow in some places. Bibliography: *CVA Pologne 5*, Pl. 34, 4—6.

Similar to No. 69, yet with short tongues above the upper foils, and below the handle a rosette in a form of four-armed star. Classification and dating as No. 69.

74. Aryballos   Pl. XXVI

MNW 148662 (purchased in 1957). H: 0.069, D: 0.066. Yellow clay. Blackish--brown glaze, yellowish-orange in some places. Glued together. Bibliography: *CVA Pologne 5*, Pl. 35, 4—6.

As No. 69, but with tongues above the upper petals. Classification and dating as No. 69.

75. Aryballos   Pl. XXVI

MNW 198027 (formerly in Silesia). H: 0.058, D: 0.056. Yellowish clay. Brownish--orange glaze. Bibliography: *CVA Pologne 5*, Pl. 34, 7—9; B e r n h a r d, Fig. 44.

Quatrefoil aryballos. Classification and dating as No. 69.

76. Aryballos   Pl. XXVI

MNW 199241 (formerly Königsberg ?). H: 0.051, D: 0.048. Yellowish clay. Brownish-red glaze, partly worn off. Missing: small fragment of mouth. Bibliography: *CVA Pologne 5*, Pl. 35, 7—9.

Quatrefoil aryballos with a strongly concave mouth surface. Decoration as in No. 69, yet the central oval linked by vertical bars with the elements connecting the upper foils. End of the 2nd quarter of the 6th cent.

Cf.: No. 69; *CVA Tübingen 1*, Pl. 27, 3—4; *CVA Mainz, Zentralmuseum 1*, Pl. 17, 8.

77. Aryballos   Pl. XXVII

MNK XI-A-347. H: 0.06, D: 0.06. Brownish-red clay. Blackish-brown glaze. Missing: great part of mouth and neck. Bibliography: P a p u c i - W ł a d y k a, No. 12.

Quatrefoil aryballos. Classification and dating as No. 76.

78. Aryballos   Pls. XXVIII, XXIX

MNW 138517 (1947, formerly Szczecin). H: 0.155, D: 0.133. Yellowish clay. Brownish-black (orange-brown in some places), mat glaze. Incisions. Glued together, partly restored. Bibliography: *CVA Pologne 5*, Pl. 31, 1—5; B e n s o n, AntK 9, 1966, p. 11 No. 6, p. 13; A m y x, CorVP, p. 244, No. A-10.

A large broad-bottomed aryballos with a ring-shaped foot and comparatively small mouth with a slightly concave rim. On the mouth surface, tongues, on the rim traces of dots. On the handle, traces of vertical zigzag. On the shoulders, tongues. On the body representation of warrior's head in a helmet shown in a r. profile, between two panthers facing each other. The painting is enclosed on both sides by double glaze stripes. Foot glazed. On the bottom circles. Not very careful workmanship. The object ranks among typical product of the closing phase of animal style and belongs to works of Winged Lion Painter. This artist has been distinguished and named by Benson (1953), who, while establishing an extended list of his works (1966), has also included the Warsaw vase, attributed to that painter by M. L. Bernhard (CVA). Late Corinthian. Winged Lion Painter (Bernhard, Benson).

Cf.: concerning Winged Lion Painter B e n s o n, GKV, p. 56, List 96; EAA 4, 1961, p. 568 (Banti); B e n s o n, AntK 9, 1966, p. 11f.; A m y x, CorVP, loc. cit.; one unpublished round aryballos with the representation of warrior's helmeted head to r. and flying bird to l. is stored in Jena (Friedrich-Schiller-Universität, Sektion Altertumswissenschaften), which, in my opinion, can be attributed to the Winged Lion Painter.

79. Aryballos   Pls. XXVIII, XXIX

MNK XI-1075 (Czartoryski coll.). H: 0.084, D: 0.084. Light yellow clay. Blackish-brown mat glaze. Incisions. Mouth slightly jagged. Bibliography: CVA Pologne 2, Pl. 3/57/1; A m y x, CorV, p. 219; id., BA Besch 38, 1963, p. 90, No. 26; G ą s i o r o w s k i, Malarstwo starożytne, Pl. 1 a; B e n s o n, GKV, p. 54, List 91, 2 (wrong information, that the object is in Gołuchów); P a p u c i - W ł a d y k a, No. 9; N e e f t, BABesch 52—53, 1978—79, p. 154, No. 10 (I owe this reference to Prof. Amyx); A m y x, CorVP, p. 238, No. A-36.

Small broad-bottomed aryballos with a ring-shaped foot and flat handle. On the mouth, concentric circles. On the rim, a representation of a swan and a panther in antithetic disposition. In the background, rosettes with wavy edges and a circle inside, and incised rosettes. On the lower body, two lines. The Cracow aryballos was adorned by an anonymous painter, who has been distinguished by Amyx (1943) and whom Benson named Herzegovina Painter (after an aryballos from Sarajevo). The earliest vases of this painter come from Middle Corinthian, but his heyday falls in the years 570—560. Late Corinthian. 570—560. Herzegovina Painter (Amyx).

Cf.: concerning Herzegovina Painter A m y x, CorV, p. 219, 230 n. 85; B e n s o n, GKV, p. 54, List 91; EAA 3, 1960, p. 434f. (Banti); A m y x, BABesch 38, 1963, p. 89—91 (enlarged list of painters' works; alabastron No. 4 from this list has been published: H o l m b e r g, P a s q u i e r, Op Ath 15, 6, 1984, p. 65—66); S e e b e r g, CorKV, p. 60, 67 n. 4; B e n s o n, Phoenix 24, 1970, p. 110; N e e f t, op. cit.; A m y x, op. cit. (see bibliography of the item); one broad-bottomed aryballos from Sindos can be, in my opinion, attributed to the painter: Σίνδος. Κατάλογος τῆς ἐκθέσης No. 420 (Thessaloniki, Museum).

80. Pyxis Pl. XXXI

MC A 3/3 (donated by Kniczek from Místek, 1846). H: 0.081 (with lid), D: 0.10. Light yellow clay. Brownish-black glaze. Red applied. Surface effaced, coarse crust in some places. Bibliography: unpublished.

Tripod-pyxis of a shape nearing to No. 57, yet with higher legs and larger, button-shaped lid lug. The lid: on the rim dots, on the upper surface and lug, circles of various diameter and a zigzag band. A thickened mouth rim: red. On the upper body and on the legs, bands of the dotted ornament in a chequered pattern, parted by wide glaze bands. Lower body, bottom and interior: undecorated. Late Corinthian. 570—525.

Cf.: on shape No. 57; CVA Heidelberg 1, Pl. 18,11 (identical decoration, similar shape); Corinth 13,1, p. 188, Pl. 88, 165-d (similar shape); Corinth 15,3, p. 251, Nos. 1394—95, Pl. 58 (similar shape and decoration).

81. Lid Pl. XXXI

MNW 198006 (formerly Silesia). H: 0.031, D: 0.126. Light yellow clay. Brownish--red glaze of wrong quality. Violet applied. Small fragment is missing; decoration partly worn off. Bibliography: unpublished.

Flat lid with a lug in the shape of a clay stripe. A plain decoration: circles of various size (some with added paint) and three series of dots between the circles. Below the lug, five slapdash tongues. Lug glazed. The lid belonged to a pyxis. The lug in form of a clay stripe is very rare. A similar lug, yet wider, is to be found on a pyxis lid from Perachora, dated to Early Corinthian. However, the decoration of the Warsaw lid corresponds with the objects dated to the Middle and Late Corinthian. Late Corinthian.

Cf.: P a y n e, Perachora 1, p. 100, Pl. 31,5; CVA Heidelberg 1, Pl. 18,7; H a y e s, Tocra 2, Nos. 1872—73, Pl. 5; T h a l m a n, Ceramique trouvée à Amathonte, [in:] G j e r s t a d, Greek Pottery, p. 81, No. 181, Pl. 18,6; Corinth 15,3, p. 291, No. 1586.

82. Amphoriskos Pl. XXXI

MNK XI-A-315. H: 0.08, D: 0.05. Light yellow clay. Blackish-brown glaze, worn off in some places. Missing: part of foot. Bibliography: CVA Pologne 2, Pl. 1/94/2.

Small vase with a large, conical foot, bulgy body strongly narrowed at the bottom, and thick, hand-made handles. Foot undecorated. On the body, stripe and in the middle, two series of dots. The shoulders decorated with tongues. On the neck and the mouth: lines. The amphoriskoi with linear decoration, composed of bands and dots, were popular in Middle Corinthian, being, however, carefully made and most often having added red. The Cracow vase, regarding its mediocre workmanship, belongs rather to the subsequent period. Late Corinthian I. 570—550.

Cf.: P a y n e, NC, p. 314, Nos. 1073ff., p. 324, Nos. 1351ff.; L o P o r t o, p. 130, complesso 62—2, Fig. 102b; U r e, AFR, p. 28, 83ff., Pl. 4: 86—261 and 99—48; B o u c h e r, CahByrsa 3, 1953, Pl. XI, 79, p. 25; *Corinth 13,1*, p. 196, gr. 188—5, Pl. 29; B e n s o n, AJA 85, 1981, p. 170, No. 1; *Corinth 15,3*, p. 293, No. 1601, Pl. 64; H a y e s, *Tocra 1*, p. 28, Nos. 21, 24, Pl. 6.

83. Cup   Pl. XXX

MNW 198003 (formerly Wrocław). H: 0.065, D: 0.213. Light yellow clay. Black (brownish-red in some places), mat glaze. Incisions. Red applied. Bibliography: *CVA Pologne 5*, Pl. 39, 1—3; A m y x, CorVP, p. 253 "Some Late Corinthian Kylixes".

Cup with an offset rim (as No. 62), yet more shallow. Interior glazed, only in its central part two circles around a dot. Mouth, handles and foot: black. On the body, an identical decoration on both sides: a bird (swan?) with its head turned back going to r. between two griffon-birds. On the birds' necks traces of red dots. Incisions sprawling and hasty. The frieze is enclosed from above by a band, and from below by stripes and bands. Decoration neglectful. The described vase, as M. L. Bernhard (*CVA*) rightly remarked, stands very near to a cup from Copenhaguen, *CVA* 2, Pl. 90,2 (= Payne,, NC, No. 1343), juxtaposed by Amyx (CorV, p. 227 n. 20) with other vases representing similar style. Basing on the observations of Amyx and adding further attributions, Benson defined this painter as Bird Frieze Painter (GKV, p. 157, List 99; AJA 60, 1956, p. 229), but Prof. Amyx, CorVP, p. 295, does not accept Benson's "Bird Frieze Painter", "which is an conglomerate, based on subject matter rather than style". Late Corinthian. 570—560.

84. Bowl   Pl. XXX

MNW 198010 (1946, formerly Wrocław). H: 0.048, D: 0.178. Yellow clay. Blackish-brown mat glaze not very good. Small injuries. Bibliography: *CVA Pologne 5*, Pl. 40, 1—2.

Shallow, thin-walled bowl having a small, ring-shaped foot and two horizontal handles of a circular cross-section. Inside, a streaky glaze. On the mouth's edge and on the handle, a narrow stripe. Below a broad band underlined with three lines. On the lower body, series of dots between the lines. Foot (also on the bottom) and a narrow stripe immediately above it: glazed. The vase belongs to the group of cups considered to descend from Greek-Oriental "bird-bowls". Late Corinthian?

Cf.: no parallel; on shape see: P a y n e, NC, p. 297ff., group B; H o p p e r, p. 227—228; D u n b a b i n, *Perachora 2*, p. 77—78.

85. Ram Pl. XXX

MNW 198017 (1945, formerly Wrocław). H: 0.062, L: 0.079. Light yellow clay. Blackish-brown glaze, almost entirely worn off. Bibliography: *CVA Pologne 5*, Pl. 42, 5,; B e r n h a r d, Fig. 64.

Plastic vase in shape of seated ram with an orifice on the head top (without neck and mouth). The animal reposes on four small, drawn-in paws. Its heavy, cylindrical and somewhat narrowed in the mid-part body has the fore part larger and the hind part smaller, with a small tail clinging to it. The neck starts almost halfway the back and turns into a small head ending in a tube-shaped snout, which narrows forwards. Large and heavy horns are fastened to the head, which are twisted spirally around an aperture (left probably by the implement used when attaching the horns). As the traces indicate, paws, tail and horns were black. Details of eyes and snout were marked. On the ram's neck and body, there were dots distributed in parallel oblique lines. From the aperture to the tail a line runs, which brings out the spine. The ram-shaped vases make one of the most numerous and widespread types of the Corinthian plastic vases. The Warsaw ram falls into the group of vessels in the form of animal with a body "en bobine" in the Ducat's classification. Late Corinthian I. 570—550.

Cf.: D u c a t, BCH 87, 1963, p. 455f., Fig. 27; R i z z o, Boll d'Arte 1960, p. 256, Fig. 16b, 1; H a y e s, *Tocra 1*, p. 155, Nos. 80—82, Pl. 103; *CVA Heidelberg 1*, Pl. 6, 3; L a u r e n s, p. 182, No. 129 (Etrusco-Corinthian); *CVA Mainz, Zentralmuseum 1*, Pl. 23, 2.

2.7. LATE CORINTHIAN II

86. Pyxis Pl. XXXI

ZAŚ UJ 10.169 (donated by W. Czartoryski, 1872). H: 0.07, D: 0.08. Light yellow clay; clay of lid: red. Black, in some places blackish-brown glaze. Fragment of lid is missing, the rest glued together. Bibliography: *CVA Pologne 2*, Pl. 5/78/3; B e r n h a r d, *Katalog*, No. 312; P a p u c i, RechACrac 1977, p. 62, No. 2, Fig. 2: C.

Pyxis has a round body with a ring-shaped foot, two horizontal, upwards directed handles, and a lid in a shape of the flattened hemisphere, with a round lug. The decoration comprises bands and two lines of dots on the shoulders. The vase represents the so-called white style and corresponds with the group of pyxides dated by Payne to Late Corinthian I. However, P. and A. Ure suggest lower dating of this group of vessels, basing on the Rhitsona finds. Late Corinthian II. 550—500.

Cf.: P a y n e, NC, p. 323, Nos. 1325—1327; *CVA Reading 1*, Pl. 6, 12 (P. and A. U r e); similar are: *CVA Copenhague 2,* Pl. 84, 8; *CVA Mainz, Universität 1,*

50

Pl. 31, 1—2; U r e, *Sixth and Fifth Century Pottery from Rhitsona*, Pl. 12: 126.82 (floral decoration); B o u c h e r, CahByrsa 3, 1953, Pl. 10, 71, p. 24 (dots on shoulders, floral decoration on body); on white style Nos. 88, 94—98.

87. Pyxis   Pl. XXXI

MDP (without inv. No.). H: 0.11, D: 0.105. Light yellow clay. Brownish-black glaze, partly worn off. Bibliography: unpublished.

Pyxis with convex sides and horizontal handles, which are directed upwards, without a lid. Mouth and the handles undecorated. Below the rim, a stripe. On the handle band, a net ornament with dots on the lines' crossings, enclosed from above by a stripe running just below the handle root. The body adorned with two bands filled with a dot--ornament in a chequered pattern between the lines, as well as bands and glazed lines. Foot glazed. Late Corinthian. 550—500.

Cf.: concerning the shape Nos. 54—56; similar bands: Nos. 80—82.

88. Pyxis   Pls. XXXII, XXXIII

MNK XI-1305 (Czartoryski coll.). H: 0.15, D: 0.135. Buff clay. Black glaze. Red for many details. White slip on women's faces and necks and on rim. Parts of lid missing, preserved parts re-assembled, decoration partly worn off. Bibliography: P a y n e, NC, p. 307, No. 894A; *CVA Pologne 2*, Pl. 3/57/4 (and the references there cited); A m y x, CorV, p. 207, 208, 215; H o p p e r, p. 219, 5; G ą- s i o r o w s k i, *Malarstwo starożytne*, Pl. 3; W a l l e n s t e i n, *Korinthische Plastik des 7. u. 6. Jhs. vor Christus*, p. 150, VII A 9; P a p u c i, RechACrac 1977, p. 63, No. 4, Fig. 1: B.

Pyxis with three handles in shape of female busts, having a flat lid with a button-shaped lug. On the lid, black and red circles. On the mouth, short strokes, distributed radially around the orifice and enclosed within lines. On the rim: zigzags. Neck: red. On the shoulders, tongues alternately black, red and reserved. Below the handle root, two series of dots between the three lines, embraced on both sides by double stripes (those marginal: red). On the lower body, three stripes (central: red). Below, two black lines. Foot: red. Busts: the women's heads adorned with high poloi painted red, except for a reserved stripe. Hairs are painted, not plastically rendered, covering a large part of the forehead, where they are set in a triangular way, while their edge remains wavy; on the sides, they come down the shoulders in a uniform mass. The women's bust, redered plastically, resemble a herm, while the women themselves are worn in red-painted clothes. In a single case, a dress displays a V-shaped low neck, through which the underlying garment is visible. Two of women have the necklaces with three pendants, one without the pendants. This latter has her upper part of the arms indicated by reserved stripes. The remaining two have no distinguished upper arms. The women's faces are elongated, with prominent straight noses, marked with glaze. Eyebrows slanting, sinking towards the outer corners of the eye, and painted. The big, bulging eyes, marked with glaze have no plastic rims. Mouths are small and narrow, with their corners directed upwards, chins protruding and distinguished. Payne placed the described vase in Middle Corinthian, while Amyx, basing upon stylistic traits of the women's heads, acknowledged it to be a work of Late Corinthian III in classification of Jenkins. Late Corinthian. 545—525. White Style (Amyx).

Cf.: J e n k i n s, BSA 32, 1931—32, p. 34f.; on shape: P a y n e, NC, p. 293, 305—307, 322, 332, Nos. 1501—1503A, very similar is No. 1501, Pl. 35, 6 and Fig. 65D; A m y x, CorV, p. 207—215: H o p p e r, p. 214—215; on white style No. 86.

89. Pyxis   Pl. XXXI

ZAŚ UJ 10.170 (donated by W. Czartoryski, 1872). H: 0.055, D: 0.075. Buff clay. Brown glaze, dark yellow in some places. Decoration heavily worn off. Bibliography: *CVA Pologne 2*, Pl. 5/78/6; H o p p e r, p. 217; B e r n h a r d, *Katalog*, No. 309; P a p u c i, RechACrac 1977, p. 63, No. 5, Fig. 2:B.

Powder-pyxis with one part entering the other. On the lid walls in the central band, an ornament of dark and light rectangles, enclosed by lines and stripes. On the top surface, a floral garland and circles. Late Corinthian. 2nd half of 6th cent. or later.

Cf.: S i e v e k i n g - H a c k l, PL. 12, 336 (= P a y n e, NC, No. 1510) analogical shape; U r e, *Sixth and Fifth Century Pottery from Rhitsona*, Pl. 12:112.31 (= P a y n e, NC, No. 1512); *CVA Gela 2*, Pl. 22, 2; *Corinth 15, 3*, p. 203f., No. 1090, Pl. 47; L a u r e n s, p. 60, No. 16 (similar central band). On shape generaly: P a y n e, NC, p. 273, No. 56, p. 293—294, Fig. 131 — No. 762, p. 333, Fig. 177. Nos. 1510—1512; H o p p e r, p. 216f.; D u n b a b i n, *Perachora 2*, p. 187—191, esp. 189—191: linear decoration.

90. Skyphos   Pl. XXXVI

MNW 198009 (formerly in Silesia). H: 0.072, D: 0.152. Light yellow clay. Black, semi-lustrous glaze. Red applied (now altered to chocolate brown). Bibliography: *CVA Pologne 5*, Pl. 40, 3; B e r n h a r d, Fig. 172.

Broad-based skyphos with a conical foot, smoothly flaring body and two large handles. Interior black, except for a stripe just below the rim. Exterior, the lip emphasised by a black line. The handles glazed on exterior. Between them, an ornament of buds alternately black and red, underlined from below by a red line. Still below, four bands, the second uppermost red. On the foot's bottom, a red band. On the vessel's bottom, three black circles. Late Corinthian. End of 6th cent. or later.

Cf.: *CVA Heidelberg 1*, Pl. 16, 6; V a n d e r p o o l, Hesperia 15, 1946, Pl. 65, 312, p. 329; *CVA Fogg Museum*, Pl. 5, 17—18; *Corinth 15, 3*, p. 188, No. 999, Pl. 44; concerning linear skyphoi see also Nos. 61, 91.

91. Skyphos Pl. XXXVI

ZAŚ UJ 10.167 (donated by M. Bodeńska). H: 0.03, D: 0.06. Light yellow clay. Blackish-brown, mat glaze. Surface effaced. Bibliography: *CVA Pologne 2*, Pl. 5/78/1; B e r n h a r d, *Katalog,* No. 314.

Miniature vase without foot, with two large handles. Between those latter, a series of zigzags. Below, two broad bands, red and black, parted by a red line. On the bottom, two black circles. Interior glazed. The skyphoi with linear decoration widespread particularly after 550 and were to be reproduced for a long time since. These vases' bodies used then to be decorated with bands, which completely supplant the rays on the lower body. The Cracow object belongs rather to the second half of the 6th cent., since its workmanship is careful, and the zigzag fills the whole height of the handle band. Late Corinthian. 2nd half of the 6th cent. or later.

Cf.: P a y n e, NC, p. 334f., No. 1517, Fig. 181B; U r e, *Sixth and Fifth Cent. Pottery from Phitsona,* p. 23, 91, 100; D u n b a b i n, *Perachora 2,* p. 296, Nos. 2949, 1947, Pl. 119; *CVA Heidelberg 1,* Pl. 16, 7.8.10—11; R o b i n s o n, H a r c u m, I l i f f e, *Catalogue of the Greek Vases in the Royal Ontario Museum,* p. 62, No. 201, Pl. 15; *CVA Sarajevo 2,* Pl. 17, 3; *CVA Mainz. Zentralmuseum 1,* Pl. 19, 12; H a y e s, *Tocra 1,* p. 40, Nos. 453ff.; *Corinth 15, 3,* Pl. 67, Nos. 1713, 1718—19; see also Nos. 61, 90.

92. Exaleiptron Pls. XXXIV, XXXV

MNW 138495 (1947, formerly Szczecin). H: 0.05, D: 0.0118. Light yellow clay. Blackish-brown glaze, yellow in some places. Glued together, small injuries, whitish crust in some spots, decoration partly worn off. Bibliography: *CVA Pologne 6,* Pl. 37, 1.3.5.

Fairly smallish vase with a high, conical foot, and an omega-shaped handle. Inside, traces of circles, also on the inverted rim. Around the orifice, two series of alternating dots between six lines. Just below the handle, a stripe. On the lower body, rays delimited by a line from above. Also, a line emphasizes the body-into-foot transition. Foot undecorated. On the bottom, traces of circles. Late Corinthian. Ca. 550.

Cf.: No. 66; P a y n e, NC, p. 335. No, 1519, Fig. 183.

93. Exaleiptron Pls. XXXIV, XXXV

MNW 198011 (1946, formerly Wrocław). H: 0.068, D: 0.191. Light yellow clay. Black, lustrous glaze. Red applied (now altered to chocolate brown). Small injuries, decoration partly worn off. Bibliography: *CVA Pologne 5,* Pl. 38, 2.4.6.

Shape as the former. On the handle, traces of glaze. Inside traces of glaze and red. On the reverted rim, a red and black stripe. Around the orifice, dots between three lines (this central: red), bordered with red stripes (three black lines on each). Foot red outside. On the bottom, red and black circels. Late Corinthian. Ca 550.

Cf.: No. 92; concerning general literature: No. 66.

94. Exaleiptron Pl. XXXIV

MNW 138009 (formerly E. Majewski Museum in Warsaw). Cumae. H: 0.055, D: 0.185. Light yellow clay. Black glaze, brownish-red in some places. Red added (now altered). Fractured, surface damaged, covered with stains, decoration worn off. Bibliography: *CVA Pologne 3*, Pl. 2/98/4; B e r n h a r d, *Wazy greckie w Muzeum im. E. Majewskiego w Warszawie*, p. 8f., No. 9, Pl. 2, 3.

Exaleiptron with a short, ring-shaped foot, a body of an ellipse cross-section and a handle as in the former case. Decoration nearing to the former, yet inside, on the handle and on the foot, traces of glaze; a dotted ornament between three lines, enclosed within two red bands; closer to the orifice, traces of a black line. Just below the handle, a black stripe. Late Corinthian. 2nd half of 6th cent. White style.

Cf.: concerning general literature see No. 66; parallels: Nos. 95—96; D u g a s, EAD 10, Pl. 36, 517—519; *CVA Hoppin Coll.*, Pl. 1, 9; *CVA Oxford 2*, Pl. 2, 30; *CVA München 3*, Pl. 145, 10; *CVA Tübingen 1*, Pl. 36, 4; *CVA Mainz, Zentralmuseum 2*, Pl. 22, 3—4; B o u c h e r, CahByrsa 3, 1953, Pls. 12, 84—85 and 13, 86; H a y e s, *Tocra 1*, Pl. 18, Nos. 249—251, 255—258, p. 34.

95. Exaleiptron Pls. XXXIV, XXXV

MNP A 8 (formerly Antiquarium, Berlin). Bari. H: 0.06, D: 0.152. Light clay with green shade. Brown glaze. Bibliography: *CVA Pologne 3*, Pl. 3/119/6 (and the references there cited); K u b c z a k, p. 171, Fig. 11; id., *Katalog*, p. 48, No. 78, Fig. 32.

Shape as the former. Decoration very similar, yet without the red colour. Differences: the upper handle edge glazed, as well as the interior, except for the central part with circles painted in it. Classification and dating as No. 94.

96. Exaleiptron Pls. XXXIV, XXXV

ZAŚ UJ 10.159 (donated by W. Czartoryski). H: 0.055, D: 0.17. Light yellow clay. Blackish-brown glaze. Red applied. Bibliography: *CVA Pologne 2*, Pl. 4/77/10; B e r n h a r d, Katalog, No. 322.

Shape as the both previously described. Decoration as No. 94, yet on the inverted rim, a red stripe within two glazed stripes. Classification and dating as No. 94.

97. Exaleiptron Pl. XXXV

MNW 198005 (1946, formerly Wrocław). H: 0.059, D: 0.174. Dark yellow clay. Brown glaze, verging on orange. Glued together. Bibliography: *CVA Pologne 5*, Pl. 37, 2.4.6.; B e r n h a r d, Fig. 71.

Shape ellipsoidal in cross-section like in the foregoing vases, yet flattened, so that the body is distinctly bent on the handle level. Foot conical, short. Decoration nearing to the preceding exaleiptron, yet the cone pattern runs around the orifice, while on the lower body (not just below the handle) there are two lines. Classification and dating as No. 94.

Cf.: *CVA Heidelberg 1*, Pl. 19,3; J u c k e r, *Aus der Antikensammlung der Bernischen Historischen Museum*, p. 34, No. 26, p. 101 n. 31; on cone pattern: P a y n e, NC, p. 287; *CVA Gela 2*, Pl. 2, 22.

98. Exaleiptron   Pl. XXXV

MNW 199229 (1948, formerly probably Königsberg). H: 0.06, D: 0.152. Yellow clay. Black glaze. Violet added. Missing: large part of body and rim. Bibliography: *CVA Pologne 5*, Pl. 38,1.3.5; this is probably the vase: L u l l i e s, p. 20, No. 26.

Shape as No. 97, yet not so flattened. Foot somewhat higher. Decoration also nearing to the former. Differences: inside, in the central part, circles against the reserved background; one of the stripes on the inverted rim: violet; around the orifice: simplified cone pattern. Foot with added colours, as well as one of the bottom circles. The described vase can be the same, which once was in Königsberg, and has been published by Lullies (see above), yet without the illustration (Inv. No. in Königsberg: F 140). The photograph of the Königsberg object has been published by Scheibler, JdI 79, 1964, p. 95, 108, Abb. 32. The description as well as the dimentions point to the identity of both vases, yet at present the vase is only fragmentarily preserved. There are also other objects from Königsberg in Warsaw (Nos. 6, 13, 17). Classification and dating as No. 94; see also No. 97 (cone pattern).

99. Exaleiptron   Pls. XXXIV, XXXV

MNW 138527 (1947, formerly Szczecin). H: 0.12, D: 0.205. Reddiah clay. Black glaze, brown in some places. Added paint: red altered to violet, and white, weakly visible. Bibliography: G r e i f e n h a g e n, AA 1936, p. 360 sub No. 16; *CVA Pologne 9*, Pl. 5, 2—3 (and the references there cited); A m y x, CerVP, p. 474, No. 4 "Stemmed Group".

Stemmed exaleiptron without handle. The vase has a cylindrical body with profiled walls, based on a high foot with a moulded ring halfway its height. On the foot's bottom, two black circles; outer surface of the foot: black; in its lower part, below the moulded ring (the latter with added paint), tongues alternately red and white. On the vertical walls, in three sequences, an ornament of black and reserved rhombi, arranged inversely in each row. On the upper surface, various, carefully made ornaments, situated in concentric stripes, parted by lines. Interior: black, only in the central part, an octofoil rosette in outline technic. Regarding the shape and decoration, two exaleiptra published by Greifenhagen stand very near to the Warsaw vase, one in Bonn, and another in Heidelberg. These two objects has been acknowledged by Greifenhagen to descend from the same workshop, and also compared with the Warsaw object (former Vogell coll.). Late Corinthian. 550—525.

Cf.: G r e i f e n h a g e n, AA 1936, Abb. 17, 19 (in Bonn) and 18 (in Heidelberg = *CVA Heidelberg 1*, Pl. 19, 7—8); S c h e i b l e r, JdI 79, 1964, p. 90, Type 4; on general literature see No. 66; on shape A m y x, CorVP, loc. cit.

100. Hydria   Pl. XXXVI

MNW 199183 (1948, formerly Frombork). H: 0.12, D: 0.09. Yellow clay. Black (brownish-red in some places), mat glaze. Red applied. Bibliography: *CVA Pologne 5*, Pl. 40, 4—7.

Small hydria with a mouth, neck, outer handles and foot glazed. On the shoulders, tongues, in an outline technic, alternately red and balck. Below, two red stripes between three black lines. Between the horizontal handles, on one side: a broken meander, on another, buds painted above dots. Still below, three bands, the central being red. Late Corinthian. 550—500 or later.

Cf.: P a y n e, NC, p. 336, No. 1533; meander pattern is typical for Late Corinthian, ibid., p. 331; buds ornament on No. 90; buds and dots on No. 101; very similar tongues on pyxis *CVA Mainz, Zentralmuseum 1*, Pl. 21, 12 and on No. 101 below.

101. Oinochoe   Pl. XXXIII

MNP IX/75/7 (deposit 1090 from Ruxer coll.). H: 0.105, D: 0.07 (bottom). Light yellowish clay. Brown, lustrous glaze. Purple paint. Missing: part of mouth. Bibliography: *CVA Pologne 3*, Pl. 1/122/4; K u b c z a k, p. 170, No. 12, Fig. 11.

Oinochoe with a high, cylindrical body, flat shoulders, narrow neck (at its base, a moulded ring, on the top, a narrowing), trefoil mouth, and high band handle. The base purple, above three bands (this central: purple), buds alternately black and purple, painted above black dots, five alternating lines of thinned glaze and purple. On the shoulders, tongues as in No. 100. Neck: purple. On the mouth and handle, traces of glaze. Late Corinthian. 2nd half of the 6th or beginning of 5th.

Cf.: P a y n e, NC, p. 336, Nos. 1542f.; *Corinth 13,3*, p. 303, No. 1652 n. 3 (on shape); similar are: *Corinth 15,3*, p. 194f., No. 1025, Pl. 45 (= N e w h a l l, AJA 35, 1931, p. 19, Fig. 17); *CVA Heidelberg 1*, Pl. 15,3; *CVA Mainz, Zentralmuseum 1*, Pl. 21, 17; D u n b a b i n, *Perachora 2*, p. 202, No. 2608, Pl. 112, No. 2606 (on dating).

102. Aryballos   Pl. XXXIII

MNW 198034. H: 0.110, D: 0.094 (bottow). Buff clay. Black lustrous glaze. Mouth and handle glued together, small restorations; numerous chips, mouth slightly jagged. Bibliography: unpublished.

Aryballos with a cylindrical body, as in No. 101, yet with more massive base and sloping shoulders; the mouth is broad, concave on both sides, with a high rim, at the neck's base: moulded ring. On the mouth rosette in outline technic on black background. On rim traces of glaze. On the shoulders, thin, densely distributed tongues. On the shoulders-into-body transition, six lines alternately black and brown. Below a double broken meander, followed by three bands (the second: brown), parted by brown lines. The lowest body and base: black. Bottom slightly concave without decoration. The body of this vase corresponds with the cylindrical oinochoai, such as e.g. No. 101, while the mouth and handle find no counterpart in the literature within my reach. The ornaments point to the late period. Late Corinthian. 550—500 or later.

Cf.: *Corinth 15,3*, p. 199, No. 1058, Pl. 46 (similar shape and decoration of body, 2nd half of 6th cent.); K o k k o u - V i r i d i, AE 1980, p. 45, No. 54, Pl. K (550—500); P e a s e, Hesperia 6, 1937, p. 284f., No. 87, Fig. 20 (460—420); on double broken meander: *Corinth 15,3*, p. 182f., No. 964, Pl. 43, p. 184, No. 977, Pl. 44, 107; *Corinth 15,2*, p. 24f.; *CVA Heidelberg 1*, Pl. 19,10; on rosette in outline on mouth: *CVA Heidelberg 1*, Pl. 12,1; *CVA Norway 1*, Pl. 2,1; H a y e s, *Tocra 1*, p. 22, Nos. 70, 72, Pl. 9.

2.8. LATE CORINTHIAN III

103. Cup
Pl. XXXVI

MNW 143223 (1952). H: 0.074, D: 0.129. Red clay. Black glaze, brown in some places. Missing: handles. Surface damaged. Bibliography: *CVA Pologne 2*, Pl. 5,1.

Cup with a short, cylindrical foot, a flattened body in a shape of the reversed cone, and high, almost vertical rim. The whole vase is black, except for the handle band with broken meander, and a stripe on a lower body. The clay colour raises doubts as to the origin of the object in Corinth workshops. Similar shape is familiar among the pottery of that centre, yet the meander ornament in the handle band has no counterpart among the vessels of that shape. Corinth? 5th or 4th cent.

Cf.: on shape: *Corinth 7,2*, p. 109, An 57, Pl. 69 (black-glazed), p. 101, An 7,8, Pl. 69, p. 80—81; L o P o r t o, complesso 76, Fig. 147e; *Corinth 14*, p. 134, No. 39, Pl. 49 (miniature); *Corinth 15,3*, No. 1491, Pl. 62; on broken meander: *Corinth 13,1*, p. 258, gr. 380—1, Pl. 61; *Corinth 15,2*, Pl. 50: XXXVI. 8,16, Pl. 48: XXXVI. 10,20; *Corinth 15, 3*, Pl. 44,46; *CVA Mainz, Zentralmuseum 1*, Pl. 21, 5—6; see also No. 100.

104. Oinochoe
Pl. XXXVI

ZAŚ UJ 10.163. H: 0.125, D: 0.10. Yellow clay. Black, mat glaze, partly effaced. Traces of red added. Mouth slightly jagged, calcareous crust on some spots. Bibliography: *CVA Pologne 2*, Pl. 4/77/14; B e r n h a r d, *Katalog*, No. 318.

Small jug with a flattened body with fairly flat shoulders, having a round mouth with high, somewhat concave rim. Neck: short, with a moulded ring at its base. Foot low. A band handle, slightly concave. The whole vase: black. The outer surface of the foot: red. Four red lines on the shoulders-into-body transition, and two on the lower body. Late Corinthian III. Round-mouthed oinochoe Type A, Group I in Palmer's classification. 1st half of 5th cent.

Cf.: *Corinth 13, 1*, p. 134—136, p. 131, Fig. 14 (Palmer); very similar are: ibid., Pl. 34: 261—2, Pl. 36: 262—6, Pl. 39: 276—2; L a u r e n s, p. 128f., Nos. 70—71.

105. Oinochoe Pl. XXXVI

ZAŚ UJ 10.160 (donated by W. Czartoryski). H: 0.135, D: 0.125. Yellow clay. Black, mat glaze. Red and white paint added. Bibliography: *CVA Pologne 2*, Pl. 4/77/11; B e r n h a r d, *Katalog*, No. 321.

Globular oinochoe with a trefoil mouth and lid. A band handle, somewhat concave in the centre. Foot conical, undecorated. The remaining parts of the vase: black. On the shoulders, equally distributed, double wavy incised lines. Below, two red lines between the three white ones. On the lower body, a red stripe. Late Corinthian III. Ca 460—450.

Cf.: P a y n e, NC, p. 337, Fig. 193, No. 1552A; *Corinth 13, 1*, p. 130—131, Fig. 14: large trefoil, p. 245, Pl. 51: 341—6, p. 236, Pl. 47: 323—3, p. 228, Pl. 42: 297—2; L a u r e n s, p. 127f., Nos. 68—69; *Corinth 15, 3*, p. 209, No. 1125, Pl. 48.

106. Oinochoe Pl. XXXVII

MNW 198083 (1946, formerly Wrocław). H: 0.13, D: 0.123. Cream-coloured clay. Black, semi-lustrous glaze, partly worn. Whitish crust on surface. Bibliography: *CVA Pologne 9*, Pl. 4, 3.

Large oinochoe with a small, conical foot, globular body, a neck narrowing slightly upwards with a moulded ring at its base, a round, strongly offset and somewhat concave mouth and a band handle, not transgressing the mouth level. On the body, deep ribs. The whole jug is glazed, except for the lower body and foot. Late Corinthian III. Round-mouthed oinochoe Type C: Ribbed in Palmer's classification. Late 5th cent.

Cf.: *Corinth 13, 1*, p. 137—138, p. 131, Fig. 14, Pl. 69: 418—2, Pl. 70: 420—5 (Palmer); *Corinth 15, 3*, p. 200, No. 1069, Pl. 46.

107. Oinochoe Pl. XXXVII

ZAŚ UJ 10.272 (donated by W. Czartoryski). H: 0.105, D: 0.095. Light yellow clay. Black, mat glaze, worn in some places. Crust on surface. Bibliography: *CVA Pologne 2*, Pl. 15/78/7; B e r n h a r d, *Katalog*, No. 323.

Shape and decoration as the former, yet the mouth more concave and the body not so broad. Classification and dating as No. 106.

Cf.: *Corinth 13, 1*, p. 275, Pl. 67: 427—9.

108. Oinochoe
Pl. XXXVII

MNW 42716 (donated by W. Semerau-Siemianowski). H: 0.104, D: 0.09. Cream-coloured clay. Brownish-grey glaze, almost entirely worn. Missing: almost whole handle. Bibliography: *CVA Pologne 3*, Pl. 1/104/14.

Shape and decoration as the former, yet the foot ring-shaped, and ribs very finely marked. The described oinochoe is somewhat later than the two foregoing ones and stands closer to the "Round-mouthed Type C: Incised" oinochoai in Palmer's classification, since the ribs are shallow, only slightly marked. Late Corinthian III. Early 4th cent.

Cf.: Nos. 106—107; *Corinth 13,1*, p. 138, p. 131, Fig. 14, p. 276, Pl. 71: 431—2, p. 277, Pl. 71: 437—2 (Palmer).

109. Oinochoe
Pl. XXXVII

MC A 9/9. H: 0.082, D: 0.095. Dark yellow clay with red shade. On large part of body coarse crust, dark-grey in colour. Bibliography: unpublished.

Squat jug, made in a blisterware technic, having a flat, broad base, without a foot. The body bent halfway its height; neck narrow, flaring, mouth round in shape and bipartite band handle. The upper body and the shoulders bear furrows having traces of scratches (made by means of fingernails?). The blisterware vases were produced in Corinth since about 450 to 146 B.C. Here come after all aryballoi and oinochoai, initially with ribs, later replaced by incised strokes and unevenly distributed blisters. Since such a decoration happens to appear in the described vase, it should be dated to the 4th cent.

Cf.: on blisterware fabric: P e a s e, Hesperia 6, 1937, p. 259, Nos. 138—143, Fig. 23; *Corinth 13,1*, p. 137—138: Round-mouthed Type C: Blisterware; S p a r k e s, T a l c o t t, *Athenian Agora 12* p. 207, Nos. 1674—1681; P e m b e r t o n, Hesperia 39, 1970, p. 300ff., Pl. 75; *Corinth 7,3*, pp. 144ff.; *Corinth 15,3*, p. 346—347; the best parallel: K a r d a r a, AJA 65, 1961, p. 265, No. 4, Pl. 81 (cited by P e m b e r t o n, op. cit., p. 301 n. 63).

110. Oinochoe
Pl. XXXVII

MNW 198030 (1946, formerly Wrocław).. H: 0.083, D: 0.065. Yellow clay. Brownish-orange glaze, mediocre in quality, worn in many places. Mouth slightly jagged. Bibliography: *CVA Pologne 9*, Pl. 4, 2.

Squat oinochoe with a false foot. Neck narrow and high, with a moulded ring at the base, and a trefoil mouth. The band handle high, slightly concave in the centre. On the handle, mouth and neck, traces of glaze. On the shoulders, petals. Below, two lines on a reserved stripe. Foot and bottom: undecorated. Late Corinthian III. Late 5th cent.

Cf.: *Corinth 15,3*, p. 184, No. 979, Pl. 44; P e a s e, Hesperia 6, 1937, p. 284f., Fig. 20, No. 91; *Corinth 14*, p. 133f., Pl. 49, 32.

111. Oinochoe Pl. XXXVII

ZAŚ UJ 10.180 (donated by W. Czartoryski). H: 0.085, D: 0.055. Dark yellow clay. Blackish-brown glaze. Red. applied. Crust in many places. Bibliography: *CVA Pologne 2*, Pl. 5/78/13; B e r n h a r d, *Katalog*, No. 303.

Small jug resembling the former, yet with a body having a shape of flattened sphere, and a foot of a smaller diameter. The whole vase is glazed, except for the shoulders, which bear the tongues. Below the handle root, two red stripes. Foot undecorated. The vase under consideration represents the same type as the former, but is later, regarding the body shape. Late Corinthian III. Fourth cent.

Cf.: W i l l i a m s, Hesperia 39, 1970, p. 5, No. 4, Pl. 1a (center and right).

112. Lekythos Pl. XXXVI

MC A 4/4.H: 0.019, D: 0.06. Light yellow clay. Black, mat glaze with olive shade, partly worn. Coarse crust in some places. Bibliography: unpublished.

Lekythos with a cylindrical body. Shoulders sloping, the neck slightly narrowed in the middle, its transition into mouth marked with a groove, a deep flaring mouth with a straight rim, a band handle attached to the shoulders and the neck. A disc-shaped, clumsy foot, with a groove below the upper edge. The mouth, neck and handle (?): glazed, like the lower body and upper surface of the foot. Shoulders and remaining part of the body: undecorated. The shape of the described vase implies its origin in the last quarter of the 5th cent. In that time, the shoulders and considerable portion of the body of such lekythoi used to be covered by white engobe, which could have also existed in the case of the Cieszyn object, yet has not survived. Late Corinthian. Last quarter of 5th cent.

Cf.: on shape: *Corinth 13, 1*, p. 141, Fig. 15, p. 143: White Ground Corinthian Group III; parallels: L a u r e n s, p. 148, Nos. 90, 92.

2.9. ITALO-CORINTHIAN

113. Oinochoe Pl. XXXVIII

MNW 138001 (formerly E. Majewski Museum in Warsaw). Cumae. H: 0.265, D: 0.111. Yellow clay, greyish-green in surface, badly baked. Black glaze, brownish--red in some places. Mouth restored. Bibliography: *CVA Pologne 3*, Pl. 2/98/6; B e r n h a r d, *Wazy greckie...*, p. 1, Pl. 1, 1; ead., Fig. 148.

High, slender jug with a small, conical foot, pear-shaped body of a high-reaching maximum diameter, relatively flat shoulders, cylindrical, high neck terminating in a trefoil mouth, and a band handle. Foot and lower body: black, except for reserved zone with two lines just

60

above the foot. Above, densely distributed lines. In the body-into-
-shoulders transition, a stripe with three groups of vertical bars. In the
central part of the neck, a band filled with an ornament of three
metopes containing two triangles with adjoining vertices, parted by
three groups of vertical bars (six in number). Mouth: black. The handle
decorated with three groups of horizontal bars. An identical mouth,
handle, and neck decoration have also the two Bern jugs, determined
by Jucker as products of Cumae workshops and dated to the 1st half
of the 7th cent. The lack of rays on the lower body of the Warsaw
vase says for its earlier dating. Italian imitation of Protocorinthian. End
of 8th — beginning of 7th cent. Probably Cumae workshop.

Cf.: J u c k e r, *Aus der Antikensammlung der Bernischen Historischen Museum*,
p. 35, No. 28—29; similar are: P o t t i e r, *Vases antiques du Louvre*, 1, Pl. 31:
D 70, p. 37; *CVA La Haye 2*, IVB, IVC, Pl. 1,2; *CVA Copenhague 2*, Pl. 93,2;
on Protocorinthian prototypes: C o l d s t r e a m, *Greek Geometric Pottery*, Pl. 21b.

114. Oinochoe   Pl. XXXVIII

MNW 147225 (formerly Wilanów). H: 0.332, D: 0.173. Reddish clay. Brownish-
-red glaze. Mouh restored. Bibliography: *CVA Pologne 9*, IVB, Pl. 44,1.

High oinochoe of a shape similar to the former one, yet with an
ovoid body. Decoration from the bottom: foot glazed, a line, seven
wide rays reaching over the body's half, a broad brown band, a reserved
stripe with groups of vertical zigzags, enclosed within lines, a single
line at the level of the lower handle root. Neck and mouth: glazed. On
the handle, two groups with six horizontal bars each. Italian imitation
of Protocorinthian. 1st half of 7th cent. Probably Cumae workshop.

Cf.: two oinochoai from Bern (see references to No. 113); F a i r b a n k s, *Catalogue of Greek and Etruscan Vases*, 1, Pl. 43, 431; S i e v e k i n g - H a c k l, Pl. 26,
615; *CVA Heidelberg 3*, Pl. 127,9 (= H a m p e *et al.*, *Sammlung des archäologischen Instituts des Universität Heidelberg*, p. 23, No. 41).

115. Oinochoe   Pl. XXXVIII

MNW 147255 (1946, formerly Wilanów). H: 0.24, D: 0.183. Yellow clay. Blackish-
-brown glaze. Traces of red added. Bibliography: *CVA Pologne 9*, Pl. 4,4.

High vase of a squat body with maximum diameter somewhat above
halfway its height. The neck narrowing upwards; trefoil mouth; thick,
bipartite handle; small, ring-shaped foot. Rim glazed; just below: an
apotropaic eye on both sides. On the shoulders, three groups of uneven
tongues. On the body, bands and stripes of various size. Neck and
mouth: glazed. Italian imitation? 2nd half of 7th cent. or later.

Cf.: R o b i n s o n, H a r c u m, I l i f f e, *Catalogue of the Greek Vases*, p. 61,
Pl. 15, 199 (Etruscan, 7th cent.); D o h a n, *Italic Tomb Group...*, p. 74ff., Nos. 17—19,
p. 108, Pl. 39 (gr. Narce 64B dated at last years of 3rd quarter and first years
of 4th quarter of 7th cent.); *CVA Mainz, Zentralmuseum 1*, Pl. 25,2 (Etruscan,

1st half of 6th cent.). Similar oinochoai were found in Crete inspired by Corinthian pottery: Coldstream, Sackett, BSA 73, 1978, p. 50ff., Nos. 3—6,
Fig. 5 (Nos. 3 and 6 with eyes at rim) dated at late 7th cent.

116. Cup Pl. XXXIX

MNW 147137 (1945, formerly Wilanów). H: 0.088, D: 0.145. Whitish clay with
pink shade. Blackish-brown glaze. Missing: part of rim and one handle (restored).
Bibliography: *CVA Pologne 5*, Pl. 40, 4.

Deep cup on a small, cylindrical foot, not distinguished from the
bottom of the vase. Mouth high, almost vertical, handles attached at
the broadest part of the body. On the mouth, traces of glaze, in the
handle band, vertical bars, on the body, two broad bands. Inside,
alternating reserved and glazed bands. The vase's clay and its decoration clearly indicate it to be a local Italian product, which originated
under the influence of imported Corinthian ware. The prototype were
the cups manufactured in Corinth in Geometric and than Protocorinthian period. Italian imitation in subgeometric tradition. 7th — early
6th cent.

Cf.: *CVA Capua, Museo Campano 4*, IIIC, Pl. 2, 4—5; Minto, NSc 1940, p. 383.
Fig. 5, 26, p. 385; Tusa, ASAtene 60, 1982, p. 200f., No. 11, Fig. 22; on Corinthian
prototypes: Coldstream, *Greek Geometric Pottery*, Pl. 18d; Johansen, Pl.
9, 4; Williams, Hesperia 40, 1971, p 27, No. 11, Pl. 7.

117. Aryballos Pl. XXXIX

MNP IX/75/5 (deposit 1092 from Ruxer coll.). H: 0.095, D: 0.055. Light yellowish
clay with greyish-brown shade. Brown, lustrous glaze. Purple applied. Bibliography: *CVA Pologne 3*, Pl. 1/122/6; Kubczak, p. 162, Fig. 1b.

Aryballos with an ovoid body. Decoration at the bottom: foot and
a narrow stripe above it: glazed, tongues (three time two apiece, one
separately), two lines, three broad bands underlined from below and
bordered from above by a series of dots and two lines. On the shoulders:
tongues; neck's base glazed. On the rim, a stripe reaching also onto
the mouth surface, where the short tongues disperse from it. A circle
around the orifice, the band handle bears three horizontal bars. Etruscan imitation of Protocorinthian style. Ca 625.

Cf.: *CVA Tours*, Pl. 18, 15 (analogous shape, similar decoration).

118. Aryballos Pl. XL

MNK XI-1064 (Czartoryski coll.). H: 0.09, D: 0.055. Light clay with pink shade.
Olive colour glaze. Red and white added. Incisions. Bibliography: *CVA Pologne 2*,
Pl. 3/57/5; Gąsiorowski, *Malarstwo starożytne*, Pl. 4a; Papuci-Władyka,
No. 14.

Pointed aryballos. The central body is occupied by a scale pattern
(single incised lines, red and white dots in scales), bordered from above

by three, and from below by two stripes. On the mouth, tongues within double circles, as well as on the shoulders and the lower body. Rim and foot: glazed. On the handle, two horizontal bars. Italo-Corinthian. Imitation of Late Protocorinthian style. Late 7th cent.

Cf.: S i e v e k i n g - H a c k l, Pl. 28, 693; A l b i z z a t i, Pl. 15, 199; *CVA Bourges*, Pl. 17; *CVA Mainz, Zentralmuseum 1*, Pl. 24, 7; on prototype see No. 13.

119. Aryballos   Pl. XL

MNK XI-A-181. H: 0.102, D: 0.058. Tan-coloured glaze. Light brown clay. Red applied. Bibliography: *CVA Pologne 2*, Pl. 1/94/6; P a p u c i - W ł a d y k a, No. 15.

Shape as the former, but a body ovoid. Decoration also nearing to No. 118, but in the central part of body: three bands; on mouth around the orifice: red circle, nearer the glazed rim is a row of short tongues. Classification and dating as No. 118.

120. Aryballos   Pl. XL

MNP A 427. H. 0.09, D: 0.047. Light clay, pinkish-grey in colour. Reddish-brown, lustrous glaze. Purple added. Numerous chips (restored), decoration partly worn. Bibliography: K u b c z a k, p. 162f., Fig. 1c; id., *Katalog*, No. 69.

Shape as the former, the body higher and more narrowed above the foot. On the body bands (with adder red), interspersed by lines. The remaining decoration elements as in No. 117, yet the tongues on the shoulders reach below the handle root. On the handle, four transverse bars. Classification as No. 118. Last quarter of 7th cent.

121. Aryballos   Pl. XL

ZAŚ UJ 10.171 (donated by W. Czartoryski, 1872). H: 0.095, D: 0.077. Dark yellow clay. Blackish-brown glaze. Red applied. Calcareous crust on some spots. Bibliography: *CVA Pologne 2*, Pl. 5/78/9; B e r n h a r d, *Katalog*, No. 308; P a p u c i - W ł a d y k a, No. 17.

Shape as No. 118. On the mouth, a red circle between the black ones. On the handle, horizontal bars. The necks's base is circumlined by a stripe, emanating the tongues of various size, which are underlined below the lower handle root. On the upper body, three broad bands (central parts in added red). Below, a broad reserved band with a black stripe running through its middle section. The lowest body and the foot: glazed. Classification as No. 118. End of 7th cent.

Cf.: *CVA Rennes*, Pl. 32, 1.

122. Aryballos   Pl. XL

ZAŚ UJ 10.172 (donated by I. Karnicki). Capri? H: 0.095, D: 0.055. Dark yellow clay. Brown glaze, partly worn. Red applied. Bibliography: *CVA Pologne 2*, Pl. 5/78/8; B e r n h a r d, *Katalog*, No. 307; P a p u c i - W ł a d y k a, No. 16.

Shape similar to No. 120. Decoration as in No. 121, yet in the broadest part of the body, four bands alternately red and brown. Classification as No. 118, dating as No. 121.

Cf.: B o u c h e r, CahByrsa 3, 1953, Pl. 16, 115, p. 29.

123. Aryballos
Pl. XL

MNK XI-1065 (Czartoryski coll.). H: 0.085, D: 0.05. Dark yellow clay. Black lustrous glaze with olive shade. Red paint directly on clay. Bibliography: *CVA Pologne 2*, Pl. 3/57/7; G ą s i o r o w s k i, *Malarstwo starożytne*, Pl. 4, b; P a p u c i-W ł a d y k a, No. 18.

Shape and decoration related to No. 122. Differences: much more slender, narrower body, the neck-into-shoulders transition emphasized by a broad stripe, on the upper body, five bands (alternately black and red). Classification and dating as No. 121.

Cf.: L a u r e n s, p. 190, No. 137; *CVA Würzburg 3*, Pl. 18, 6; *CVA Rennes*, Pl. 32, 2.

124. Aryballos
Pl. XL

MNW 199420 (1948, Minutoli coll.). H: 0.082, D: 0.05. Yellow clay with red shade. Brownish-red glaze, yellow in some places. Red applied. Missing: mouth, handle and neck. Bibliography: unpublished.

The body shape as in the former vase, yet with a stronger narrowing above the foot, which is very intensively distinguished. Decoration also nearing, yet below the tongues, three glazed lines, then five bands (three red and two glazed). Classification and dating as No. 121.

Cf.: *CVA Copenhague 2*, Pl. 94, 2; *CVA Limoges*, Pl. 19, 14.

125. Aryballos
Pl. XL

MNP A 400. H: 0.09, D: 0.05. Yellowish clay with greyish-brown shade. Brown lustrous glaze. Purple paint. Missing: part of rim and foot. Bibliography: K u b c z a k, p. 161f., Fig. 1a; id., *Katalog*, No. 68, Fig. 28.

Shape as No. 122, foot as No. 124. Decoration of the shoulders, mouth and handle as in No. 120. On the upper body, slanting parallel bars enclosed within two lines. This ornament is framed on sides by broader stripes (with added purple in the centre). Above, two lines. The lower body's decoration as on the former vase. Classification and dating as No. 121.

Cf.: *CVA Como, Civico Museo Archeologico "Giovo"*, Pl. 5, 6, *CVA Rennes*, Pl. 32, 3; *CVA Limoges*, Pl. 19, 13; *CVA Tours*, Pl. 18, 16.

126. Aryballos
Pl. XLI

MNK XI-1419 (Czartoryski coll.). H: 0.089, D: 0.048. Dark yellow clay. Blackish--brown, mat glaze. Red applied. Mouth slightly jagged. Bibliography: *CVA Pologne 2*, Pl. 3/57/6; P a p u c i - W ł a d y k a, No. 19.

Shape as the former, yet more flattened shoulders and the body's maximum diameter falls higher. On the upper body a herring-bone pattern between the bands (with red applied). Below, three lines against the background of the reserved band. The remaining decoration nearing to the former. Classification as No. 121. End of the 7th cent. or later.

Cf.: *CVA Bruxelles 3*, Pl. 2, 15; *CVA Capua, Museo Campano 4*, Pl. 5, 9; L a u r e n s, Pl. 190, No. 138; *CVA Bourges*, Pl. 17, 4.

127. Aryballos   Pl. XLII

MNW 198528 (1946, formerly Wrocław). H: 0.075, D: 0.055. Dark yellow clay with red shade. Brownish-olive, semi-lustrous glaze. Red applied. Bibliography: *CVA Pologne 9*, Pl. 4, 1.

Vase of a very rare form. In its upper part, it proves to be a typical pointed aryballos (cf. Nos. 117—126), which however, bands halfway the body, and assumes a shape of the flattened sphere based on a low, ringshaped foot. The upper part decoration as in aryballoi Nos. 121 and 124. On the round protion of the body, bands red and glaze-coloured, also one reserved, filled with vertical strokes; the lowest body is decorated by two lines. Foot: glazed. Italian (Etruscan?) imitation. 1st quarter of 6th cent.

Cf.: analogous shape: *CVA Louvre 9*, Pl. 4, 14; similar shape and decoration: *CVA Bruxelles 3*, III Cb. Pl. 2, 6; M i n g a z z i n i, *Catalogo Coll. Castellani*, Pl. 31, 6.

128. Aryballos   Pl. XLII

MNK XI-A-180. H: 0.073, D: 0.051. Light brown clay with red shade. Brownish--red glaze. Bibliography: *CVA Pologne 2*, Pl. 1/94/7; P a p u c i - W ł a d y k a, No. 26.

This vase gives the impression as if it were composed of two parts. The upper one is a typical pointed aryballos, while the lower appears to be a bowl based on a broad, short foot. On the mouth, circles. On the flat handle, two horizontal bars. On the shoulders, thick tongues. Below, a brownish line. The body of the aryballos is taken by a glaze band with three groups of short vertical strokes above it. The "bowl's" rim and foot: glazed. From the foot upwards, thick tongues come out (in four groups with two in each). Italian imitation. Later than the beginning of the 6th cent.

Cf.: similar decoration of upper part: S i e v e k i n g - H a c k l, Pl. 29, 755.

129. Aryballos   Pl. XXXIX

MNP A 401. H: 0.075, D: 0.067. Light clay, greyish-brown in colour. Brown, semi-lustrous glaze. Purple applied. Missing: part of mouth, small injuries. Bibliography: K u b c z a k, p. 164, Fig. 3; id., *Katalog*, No. 70, Fig. 29.

Round aryballos with a flattened body. On the mouth, circles (one of them: purple). On the handle, two horizontal bars. On the shoulders, elongated tongues. Rim glazed. On the body, two glazed bands parted by a purple stripe. On the bottom a painted inscription (see Pl. XXXIX) acknowledged by Kubczak to be original, which, however, is hardly conceivable for me. Etruscan imitation of Early Corinthian style. 1st half of the 6th century.

Cf.: Sieveking-Hackl, Pl. 29, 746; Albizzati Pl. 14, 209; *CVA Capua, Museo Compano 4*, III C, Pl. 4, 2; Boucher, CahByrsa 3, 1953, Pl. 18, 128 and 133, p. 31; Fairbanks, *Catalogue of Greek Vases*, Pl. 42, 410; *CVA Tours*, Pl. 18. 7.9.11; *CVA Bourges*, Pl. 17, 12; *CVA Rennes*, Pl. 32, 5.6.7. (with parallels and considerations on dating of this type of vases). On prototypes: Payne, NC, p. 291, No. 642.

130. Alabastron
Pl. XLI

ZAS UJ 10.173. H: 0.11, D: 0.065. Yellowish-brown clay. Blackish-brown glaze. Red added. Bibliography: *CVA Pologne 2*, Pl. 5/78/11; Bernhard, *Katalog*, No. 305; Papuci-Władyka, No. 21.

Alabastron squat in shape, which ensues from the disproportionally broad lower body (flattened on the bottom) to the narrow neck. Handle and mouth: small. On the mouth, a red circle; on the rim, glazed strip. On the shoulders, elongated tongues. On the body, a broad band filled with dots, which are framed from above and below by broad glazed bands with added paint in middle parts. Etrusco-Corinthian. Late 7th — early 6th cent.

Cf.: Cook, Butchard, BSR 17, 1949, p. 1, No. 4, Pl. 1b; *CVA Bourges*, IVB, Pl. 17. 10.11.13; *CVA Tours*, IVBc Pl. 18, 12; Laurens, p. 193, No. 140; *CVA Rennes*, Pl. 33, 6; *CVA Mainz, Zentralmuseum 1*, Pl. 24, 12; *CVA Würzburg 3*, Pl. 18, 3; on dating of this type of alabastra: *CVA Budapest 1*, Pl. 12, 1; *CVA Rennes*, Pl. 33, 3. On prototypes see Nos. 19—21.

131. Alabastron
Pl. XLI

MNK XI-A-317. H: 0.076, D: 0.043. Dark yellow clay with brown shade. Blackish-brown glaze. Red for details. Decoration heavily worn. Bibliography: *CVA Pologne 2*, Pl. 1/94/5; Papuci-Władyka, No. 22.

Shape and decoration as in No. 130, except for longer and narrower tongues on the shoulders. Classification and dating as No. 130.

132. Alabastron
Pl. XLII

MAK AS/3591. Pantikapaion. H: 0.08, D: 0.04. Dark yellow clay. Blackish--brown glaze. Missing: mouth and part of neck. Bibliography: *CVA Pologne 2*, Pl. 4/93/6; Papuci-Władyka, No. 23.

Shape and decoration as the former as well as classification and dating.

Cf.: Laurens, No. 141; *CVA Rennes*, Pl. 33, 3.

133. Alabastron
Pl. XXXIX

MAK AS/3457/14. From Carnuntum? H· 0.06, D: 0.035. Dark-yellow clay. Brown glaze. Calcareous crust on some spots. Bibliography: *CVA Pologne 2*, Pl. 4/93/5; N o l l, Anzeiger der phil.-hist. Klasse der Österreichische Akademie der Wissenschaften 114, 1977, No. 13, p. 282 n. 6 (concerning the doubtful provenience of this object); P a p u c i - W ł a d y k a, No. 24.

Shape like No. 131, decoration nearing, yet the tongues start from the handle root and reach to the first band on the body; four dots on the handle. Classification and dating as No. 130.

134. Alabastron
Pl. XLI

ZAŚ UJ 10.177 (donated by W. Czartoryski). H: 0.06, D: 0.035; Greyish-yellow clay. Blackish-brown glaze. Red added. Mouth partly damaged. Bibliography: *CVA Pologne 2*, Pl. 5/78/14; B e r n h a r d, *Katalog*, p. 106, No. 199; P a p u c i - - W ł a d y k a, No. 25.

Shape as the former, but a relatively broad neck has two moulded rings and the handle is considerably larger, clearly distinguished and remote from the alabastron's neck. On the mouth, two red circles; its rim glazed. Below the lower ring, a stripe runs, from which long and thin tongues come out downwards. On the body, two series of large dots, parted by three lines, bordered from above and below by broader bands (with added red). On the handle, horizontal bars. Etrusco-Corinthian. End of the 7th — 1st half of the 6th cent.

Cf.: C o o k, B u t c h a r d, BSR 17, 1949, p. 1, Pl. 1a, No. 6; *CVA Tours*, Pl. 18, 10; *CVA Limoges*, Pl. 19, 7; *CVA Louvre 9*, Pl. 2, 10—20; L a u r e n s, p. 195, No. 142; *CVA Würzburg 3*, Pl. 18, 4; *CVA Rennes*, Pl. 33, 2 (with further examples and considerations about dating).

135. Alabastron
Pl. XLI

MNW 228051 (1969, Madeyski coll.). H: 0.075, D: 0.04. Dark yellow clay with pinkish shade. Blackish-brown glaze. Red added. Bibliography: unpublished.

Shape as No. 134, yet not so squat. On the mouth, a red circle. Decoration in the upper part as in the case of the former alabastron. Below the tongues, a line and then five bands alternately glazed and red, situated close one to another. The lowest body, left reserved, is cut by a narrower glazed stripe. Etrusco-Corinthian, 1st half of the 6th cent.

Cf.: *CVA Copenhague 2*, Pl. 94, 14; *CVA Rhode Island School of Design*, Pl. 5, 6; B e a z l e y, M a g g i, *La raccolta B. Gugliemi*, p. 73, No. 83, Pl. 27; F a i r b a n k s, *Catalogue of Greek Vases*, Pl. 42, No. 409; *CVA Bruxelles 3*, IIICb, Pl. 2, 8—9; *CVA Mainz, Zentralmuseum 1*, Pl. 24, 9.

136. Alabastron
Pl. XLI

MDP. H: 0.082, D: 0.05. Dark yellow clay with red shade. Blackich-brown glaze. Crust in many places. Bibliography: unpublished.

Shape as No. 134, yet the bottom more round. On the mouth, short tongues between two circles, rim: glazed. On the body, an ornament composed of five groups of parallel, slightly slanting lines, embraced on both sides by broad glazed bands (with added red in the centre). This decorative zone is enclosed from above by two lines, and from below by one, more remote from it. Classification and dating as No. 134.

Cf.: *CVA Louvre 9*, Pl. 2, 21; *CVA Limoges*, Pl. 19, 6; *Bruxelles 3*, IIICb—IVB, Pl. 2, 16.

137. Alabastron

Pl. XLIII

MNP A 9 (formerly Antiquarium, Berlin). Nola. H: 0.15, D: 0.065. Light greyish clay with pink shade. Brown, lustrous glaze. Purple for details. Incisions. Missing: small part of mouth. Bibliography: *CVA Pologne 3*, Pl. 3/119/7; K u b c z a k, p. 166, Fig. 6a—b; A m y x, [in:] *Studi in onore di Luisa Banti*, p. 13, No. 11; K u b c z a k, *Katalog*, No. 76, Fig. 31.

Fairly large, slender alabastron with a small handle. On the mouth, three circles, on the rim, dots. On the handle, two transverse bars and a dot. On the upper body, tongues; two friezes between the glazed stripes. Upper frieze: two cocks, between them two rosettes. Lower frieze: two panthers facing the central "tree". In the background of both friezes, various filling ornaments. The described vase was adorned, according to Amyx, by an artist named "Tree Painter", regarding the ornament resembling the tree, which frequently happens to occur between the animals facing each other. However, Szilágyi speaks of "Cycle des coqs affrontés", and Tree Painter is the outstanding personality in this Cycle. The artist in question is exceptionally prolific (more than 60 attributed vases) yet he fails to display more ingeniousness. In my opinion, an alabastron fragment with cocks from Populonia should be added to the list of his works, as well as two alabastra preserved intact, one in Carthage, and another in Tours. Etrusco-Corinthian. 590—550. Tree Painter (Amyx).

Cf.: A m y x, [in:] *Studi on onore...*, p. 12—24, Pl. 2b—c; id., St. Etr 35, 1967, p. 108—110; A l b i z z a t i, p. 50; S z i l á g y i, RA 1972, p. 123ff., Fig. 13; *CVA Budapest 1*, p. 38f., Pl. 10, 1—7 (Szilágyi); M i n t o, NSc 1940, p. 383, Fig. 5, 22 (fragment from Populonia); B o u c h e r, CahByrsa 3, 1953, Pl. 16, 117, p. 30 (vase from Carthage); *CVA Tours 1*, Pl. 17, 1—4.

138. Olpe

Pl. XLIV

MNW 147820 (purchased in 1950). H: 0.371, D: 0.174. Light brown clay. Blackish-brown glaze. Red and white for details. Incisions. Glued together. Bibliography: *CVA Pologne 9*, Pl. 43, 1—4; D o b r o w o l s k i, *Sztuka Etrusków*, Fig. 43.

Jug with a short, ring-shaped foot, a body narrowing upwards and terminating in a moulded ring, which separates it from the neck. The neck flares, and makes a transition into mouth of a large diameter (almost equal to the maximum body width) and having an offset, downwards everted rim. The massive, tripartite handle has two discs attached to its upper root. The handle, discs, mouth and neck: black. On the neck, traces of four-dotted rosette with the dots linked by a cross. On the body: four animal friezes, parted by a black bands with added red, and framed by two white lines. The animals are represented in a monotonous way, all of them facing r. They are lions, panthers, bucks and swans, clumsily painted. The incisions at times come to be a decorative motif, e.g. in the shoulders area they assume a shape of a single or double circle, losing completely their functional character. In the background of all the friezes, there is a dense filling ornament: incised rosettes of various shapes and large dots. On the lower body, rays. Foot glazed. The Warsaw vase belongs to Olpai Cycle, distinguished by Szilágyi from Group of Vatican 127. This scholar classified the olpe under consideration with Herclé Group, one of the groups within the frames of the Cycle. On the other hand Bernhard attributes the said vase to Queen's College Painter, associated with Herclé Group. Prof. Amyx write (in private letter August 26, 1987): "I believe it is Szilágyi's intention to have this lot (i.e. Queen's College Painter) absorbed by the Herclé Painter. Cf. Szilágyi, Etruszko Korinthosi Vazafesteszet, Budapest 1975, pp. 113—119". Etrusco-Corinthian. 590—560. Herclé Painter (Szilágyi). Queen's College Painter (Bernhard).

Cf.: S z i l a g y i, ArchCl 20, 1968, p. 15 n. 37; A m y x, [in:] *Studi in onore...,* p. 6 (Group of Vatican 127); id., StEtr 36, 1967, p. 105, Pl. 40.

3. BIBLIOGRAPHY

I use the abbrevations according to the American Journal of Archaeology and Archäologische Bibliographie. After the Polish title of publication, the title of the summary in foreign language (only when existing) is given in brackets.

Albizzati — C. Albizzati, *Vasi antichi dipinti del Vaticano*, Rome 1924.

Amyx, CorV — D. A. Amyx, *Corinthian Vases in the Hearst Collection at San Simeon*, University of California Publications in Classical Archaeology, 1, No. 9, Berkley—Los Angeles 1943, pp. 207—240.

D. A. Amyx, *The Geladakis Painter*, Hesperia 25, 1965, pp. 72—77.

D. A. Amyx, *An Alabastron by the Herzegovina Painter*, BABesch 38, 1963, pp. 89—91.

D. A. Amyx, *Some Etrusco-Corinthian Vase Painters*, [in:] *Studi in onore di Luisa Banti*, Rome 1965, p. 1—14.

D. A. Amyx, *The Mingor Painter and others: Etrusco-Corinthian, Addenda,* StEtr 35, 1967, pp. 87—111.

D. A. Amyx, Gnomon 41, 1969, p. 682f.

D. A. Amyx, *Observations on the Warrior Group*, CSCA 2, 1969, pp. 1—25.

D. A. Amyx, *Dodwelliana*, CSCA 4, 1971, pp. 1—48.

D. A. Amyx, see *Corinth* 7, 2.

Amyx, CorVP — D. A. Amyx, *Corinthian Vase-Painting of the Archaic Period* (in print).

D. A. Amyx, P. Lawrence, *Adversaria Critica — In and Around the Sphinx Painter*, AJA 68, 1964, pp. 387—390.

J. K. Anderson, *Old Smyrna: The Corinthian Pottery*, BSA 53—54, 1958—59, pp. 138—151.

T. Bakir, *Der Kolonnettenkrater in Korinth und Attica zwischen 625 und 550 vor Chr.*, Beiträge zur Archäologie 7, Würzburg 1974.

J. D. Beazley, rev. of *CVA Pologne 1*, JHS 52, 1932, p. 142.

J. D. Beazley, F. Maggi, *La raccolta Benedetto Gugliemi nel Museo Gregoriano Etrusco*, 1, Rome, Città del Vaticano 1939.

Benson, GKV — J. L. Benson, *Geschichte der Korinthischen Vasen*, Basel 1953.

J. L. B e n s o n, *Some Notes on Corinthian Vase Painters*, AJA 60, 1956, pp. 219—230.

J. L. B e n s o n, *Corinthian Vases at Wellesley College*, AJA 68, 1964, p. 167ff.

J. L. B e n s o n, *The Winged Lion Painter*, AntK 9, 1966, pp. 2—15.

J. L. B e n s o n, *Corinthian Vases in Montreal and Saint John*, Phoenix 24, 1970, pp. 106—111.

J. L. B e n s o n, *A Floral Master of the Chimaera Group: The Otterlo Painter*, AntK 14, 1971, pp. 13—24.

J. L. B e n s o n, *Corinthian Vases at Rouen*, AJA 85, 1981, pp. 169—173.

J. L. B e n s o n, *Corinthian Kotyle Workshop*, Hesperia 52, 1983, pp. 311—326.

J. L. B e n s o n, see *Corinth* 15, 3.

S. B e n t o n, *Excavations in Ithaca*, BSA 39, 1938—39, pp. 1—51.

M. L. B e r n h a r d, *Wazy greckie w Muzeum im. E. Majewskiego WTN w Warszawie*, Prace Zakładu Archeologii Klasycznej Uniwersytetu im. J. Piłsudskiego, 1 (with a French "Résumé"), Warszawa 1936.

M. L. B e r n h a r d, *Stanisław Kostka Potocki, kolekcjoner waz greckich*, Meander 6, 1951, pp. 430—449.

B e r n h a r d — M. L. B e r n h a r d, *Greckie malarstwo wazowe*, Warszawa 1966.

M. L. B e r n h a r d, *Krakowskie zbiory starożytności (Collections of Ancient Art in Cracow)*, Rozprawy i Sprawozdania Muzeum Narodowego w Krakowie, 10, 1970, pp. 7—19.

B e r n h a r d, *Katalog* — M. L. B e r n h a r d, ed., *Zabytki archeologiczne Zakładu Archeologii Śródziemnomorskiej Uniwersytetu Jagiellońskiego. Katalog*, Warszawa—Kraków 1976.

K. B i e l e n i n, *XX-lecie działalności Muzeum Archeologicznego w Krakowie (1945—1963)*, Materiały Archeologiczne 6, 1965, pp. 215—225.

C. W. B l e g e n, see *Corinth* 13, 1.

E. B o u c h e r, *Céramique archaïque d'importation au Musée Lavigerie de Carthage*, CahByrsa 3, 1953, p. 11ff.

J. K. B r o c k, *Excavations at Siphnos*, BSA 44, 1949, p. 51ff.

C. B r o k a w, *The Dating of the Protocorinthian Kotyle*, [in:] *Essays in Memory of Karl Lehman* (Marsyas Suppl. 1), 1964, p. 49ff.

L. B r o ż e k, *Z dziejów muzealnictwa w Cieszynie*, Rocznik Muzeum Górnośląskiego w Bytomiu. Historia, Fasc. 1, Bytom 1963, p. 15ff.

R. M. B u r r o w s, P. N. U r e, *Kothons and Vases of Allied Types*, JHS 31, 1911, pp. 72—99.

C. B. R. B u t c h a r d, R. M. C o o k, *Some Bucchero vases from Ardea (Latium)*, BSR 17, 1949, pp. 1—2.

F. C a n c i a n i, *Aus der Heidelberger Universitätssammlung*, AA 1963, col. 556—566.

D. C a l l i p o l i t i s - F e y t m a n s, *Origine de la pyxis convexe et sans anses à Corinth*, AE 1973, pp. 1—18.

D. C a l l i p o l i t i s - F e y t m a n s, *Origine du cratère à colonettes*, BCH 101, 1977, pp. 235—239.

J. C h i t t e n d e r, *The Master of Animals*, Hesperia 16, 1947, pp. 89—114.

J. N. C o l d s t r e a m, *Greek Geometric Pottery. A Survey of Ten Local Styles and Their Chronology*, London 1968.

J. N. C o l d s t r e a m, L. H. S a c k e t t, *Knossos: Two Deposits of Orientalizing Pottery*, BSA 73, 1978, p. 50ff.

R. M. C o o k, *A Note on the Absolute Chronology of th Eight and Seventh Centuries B.C.*, BSA 64, 1969, pp. 13—15.

R. M. C o o k, see C. B. R. B u t c h a r d.

Corinth. The Results of Excavations conducted by the American School of Classical Studies at Athens:

Corinth 7,1. S. S. W e i n b e r g, *The Geometric and Orientalizing Pottery,* Cambridge Mass. 1943.

Corinth 7,2. D. A. A m y x, P. L a w r e n c e, *Archaic Corinthian Pottery and the Anaploga Well,* Princeton 1975.

Corinth 7,3. R. E d w a r d s, *Corinthian Hellenistic Pottery,* Princeton 1975.

Corinth 13,1. C. W. B l e g e n, H. P a l m e r, R. S. Y o u n g, *The North Cemetery,* Princeton 1964.

Corinth 14. C. R o e b u c k, *The Asklepieion and Lerna,* Princeton 1951.

Corinth 15,2. A. N. S t i l l w e l l, *The Potters' Quarter. The Terracottas,* Princeton 1952.

Corinth 15,3. J. L. B e n s o n, A. N. S t i l l w e l l, *The Potters' Quarter. The Pottery,* Princeton, New Jersey 1984.

C. D e h l, *Die Korinthische Keramik des 8. und frühen 7. Jhs. v. Chr. in Italien. Untersuchungen zu ihrer Chronologie und Ausbreitung,* Berlin 1984.

W. D o b r o w o l s k i, *Sztuka Etrusków,* Warszawa 1971.

W. D o b r o w o l s k i, *Poglądy Stanisława Kostki Potockiego na wazy greckie w świetle opinii współczesnych,* Biuletyn Historii Sztuki 34, 1972, p. 168—177.

E. H. D o h a n, *Italic Tomb Group in the University Museum (of Philadelphia),* Philadelphia 1942.

J. D u c a t, *Les vases plastiques corinthiens,* BCH 87, 1963, pp. 431—458.

J. D u c a t, *Les vases plastiques rhodiens archaïques en terre cuite,* Paris 1966.

Ch. D u g a s, EAD 10, *Les vases de l'Héraion,* Paris 1928.

D u n b a b i n, *Perachora 2* — T. J. D u n b a b i n et al., *Perachora. The Sanctuaries of Hera Akraia and Limenia,* Vol. 2: *Pottery, Ivories, Scarabs and other Objects from the Votiv Deposit of Hera Limenia,* Oxford 1960.

T. J. D u n b a b i n, M. R o b e r t s o n, *Some Protocorinthian Vase-Painters,* BSA 48, 1953 (publ. 1954), pp. 172—181.

R. E d w a r d s, see *Corinth 7,3.*

A. F a i r b a n k s, *Catalogue of Greek and Etruscan Vases, 1: Early Vases Preeceding Athenian Black-Figured Ware,* Museum of Fine Arts, Boston, Cambridge Mass. 1928.

S. J. G ą s i o r o w s k i, *Malarstwo starożytne w zbiorach Czartoryskich w Krakowie. Wybór zabytków,* Kraków 1952.

G j e r s t a d, *Greek Pottery* — E. G j e r s t a d et al., *Greek Geometric and Archaic Pottery Found in Cyprus,* Acta Instituti Atheniensis Regni Sueciae, Series 4, Vol. 26, Stockholm 1977.

L. G r a b o w s k i, *Muzeum Diecezjalne w Płocku. Informator,* Płock 1972.

A. G r e i f e n h a g e n, *Ausserattische schwarzfigurige Vasen im akademischen Kunstmuseum zu Bonn,* AA 51, 1936, p. 346.

R. H a c k l, see S i e v e k i n g J.

R. H a m p e et al., *Sammlung des archäologischen Instituts der Universität Heidelberg,* 2, Mainz 1971.

C. H a r c u m, see D. R o b i n s o n.

H a y e s, *Tocra 1* and *2* — J. H a y e s, J. B o a r d m a n, *Excavations at Tocra, 1963—65, 1: The Archaic Deposit I,* London 1966. *2: The Archaic Deposits II and Later Deposits,* London 1973.

H. H o f f m a n, *Erwerbungen der Antiken Abteilung 1961—1963,* JbHambKuSamml 8, 1963, p. 214f.

E. J. H o l m b e r g, A. P a s q u i e r, *Four Corinthian Vases in the Röhs Museum and Some others,* Op Ath 15, 1984, pp. 52—66.

72

Hopper — R. J. Hopper, *Addenda to "Necrocorinthia"*, BSA 44, 1949, pp. 162—257.

C. Illife, see D. Robinson.

R. J. H. Jenkins, *Archaic Argive Terracotta Figurines to 525 B.C.*, BSA 32, 1931—32, pp. 24—40.

Johansen — K. F. Johansen, *Les vases sicyoniens*, Paris 1923.

H. Jucker, *Aus der Antikensammlung der Bernischen Historischen Museum*, Bern 1970.

Ch. Kardara, *Dyeing and Weaving Works at Isthmia*, AJA 65, 1961, p. 265.

K. Kokkou-Viridi, Συλλογή ἀγγείων τού πανεπιστημίου' Αθηνῶν, AE 1980, pp. 33—61.

S. Komornicki, *Muzeum Książąt Czartoryskich* (Muzea Polskie 5), Kraków 1929, pp. 3—8.

Kubczak — J. Kubczak, *Naczynia greckie o stylu orientalizującym w zbiorach poznańskich (Les vases corinthiens et italo-corinthiens, faisant partie des collections de Poznań)*, Archeologia 11, 1959—60, pp. 161—174.

Kubczak, *Katalog* — J. Kubczak, ed., *Zbiory starożytności Muzeum Narodowego w Poznaniu. Katalog wystawy* (with an English "Summary"), Poznań 1983.

K. Kübler, *Kerameikos 5,1 : Die Nekropole des 10. bis 8. Jahr.* Berlin 1954.

K. Kunisch, *Antiken der Sammlung C. Julius und Margot Funcke*, 1972.

Laurens — A. F. Laurens, *Céramique corinthienne et étrusco-corinthienne*, Societé Archéologique de Montpellier, Catalogue des collections 1, Montpelier 1974.

P. Lawrence, *The Corinthian Chimaera Painter*, AJA 63, 1959, pp. 348—363.

P. Lawrence, see D. A. Amyx.

P. Lawrence, see *Corinth 7, 2*.

Lo Porto — G. T. Lo Porto, *Ceramica arcaica delle necropoli di Taranto*, ASAtene 37—38, 1959—1960, p. 7ff.

S. S. Lukesh, *A New Corinthian Painter: The St. Raymond Painter*, AJA 84, 1980, pp. 184—186.

Lullies — R. Lullies, *Antike Kleinkunst in Königsberg*, Königsberg 1935.

R. Lullies, *Eine Sammlung griechischer Kleinkunst*, Munich 1955.

R. Lullies, *Antike Kunstwerke aus der Sammlung Ludwig, 1: Frühe Tonsarkophage und Vasen*, Mainz 1980.

J.-J. Maffre, *Vases grecs de la collection Zénon Piéridès*, BCH 95, 1971, p. 624ff.

F. Maggi, see J. D. Beazley.

K. Michałowski, *Sztuka starożytna*, Warszawa 1955.

P. Mingazzini, *Catalogo dei vasi della Collezione Castellani*, Rome 1930.

P. Mingazzini, *La datazione della ceramica protocorinzia e di altre ceramiche arcaiche*, MemAccLinc, Series 8, Vol 19, Fasc. 4, Rome 1976.

A. Minto, *Reggione VII (Etruria). III: Populonia*, NSc 1940, pp. 375—397.

Muzeum Narodowe w Krakowie. Zbiory Czartoryskich. Historia i wybór zabytków (also an English, French and German eds.), Warszawa 1979.

C. Neeft, BABesch 52—53, 1978—79, p. 154ff.

A. E. Newhall, *The Corinthian Kerameikos*, AJA 35, 1931, pp. 1—30.

R. Noll, *Ein unbekanntes Mithrasrelief und andere Funde aus "Carnuntum" in Krakau*, Anzeiger der phil.-hist. Klasse der Österreichischen Akademie der Wissenschaften 114, 1977, No. 13, p. 282, n. 6.

H. Palmer, see *Corinth 13, 1*.

E. Papuci, *Corinthian Pyxides in Cracow's Collections*, RechACrac 1977, Kraków 1978, pp. 59—64.

Papuci-Władyka — E. Papuci-Władyka, *Corinthian Alabastra and Aryballoi from the Cracow Collections*, PraceA 29, Kraków 1980, pp. 39—57.

E. Papuci, *Wazy korynckie w Polsce, 1: Historia badań*, Studia Archeologiczne 2, Warszawa 1984, pp. 17—27.

E. Papuci-Władyka, *An Aryballos of Bestum Painter*, RechACrac 1983, Kraków 1985, pp. 70—72.

E. Papuci-Władyka, *Aryballos Malarza Bestum w Krakowie (De aryballo antiquo in Musaeo Cracoviensi asservato)*, Meander 40, 1985, pp. 194—195.

A. Pasquier, see E. J. Holmberg.

Payne, NC — H. G. G. Payne, *Necrocorinthia. A Study of Corinthian Art in the Archaic Period*, Oxford 1931.

Payne, PV — H. G. G. Payne, *Protokorinthische Vasenmalerei (Bilder Griechischer Vasen)*, Berlin 1933 (repr. 1975).

Payne, *Perachora 1* — H. G. G. Payne et al., *Perachora. The Sanctuaries of Hera Akraia and Limenia*, vol. 1: *Architecture, Bronzes, Terracottas*, Oxford 1940.

M. Z. Pease, *A Well of the Late Fifth Century at Corinth*, Hesperia 6, 1937, pp. 257—316.

E. G. Pemberton, *The Vrysoula Classical Deposit from Ancient Corinth*, Hesperia 39, 1970, pp. 265—307.

F. Perdrizet, FdD 5,1: *Monuments figurés. Petits bronzes, terres cuites, antiquités diverses*, Paris 1908.

E. Pottier, *Vases antiques du Louvre*, Paris 1897—1901.

G. Rizza, *Boll d'Arte 45*, 1960, p. 256ff.

R. Robinson, C. Harcum, J. Illiffe, *Catalogue of the Greek Vases in the Royal Ontario Museum of Archaeology*, Toronto 1930.

C. Roebuck, see *Corinth 14*.

L. H. Sackett, see J. N. Coldstream.

I. Scheibler, *Exaleiptra*, JdI 79, 1964, pp. 72—108.

I. Scheibler, *Kothon, exaleiptron. Addenda*, AA 1968 (publ. 1968—69), pp. 389—397.

Seeberg, CorKV — A. Seeberg, *Corinthian Kômos Vases*, University of London, Institute of Classical Studies, Bulletin Supplement No. 27, London 1971.

A. Seeberg, *The Wellcome Painter and his Companions*, ActaA 35, 1964 (publ. 1965), pp. 29—50.

Sieveking-Hackl — J. Sieveking, R. Hackl, *Die königliche Vasensammlung zu München*, München 1912.

Σίνδος. Κατάλογος τῆς ἐκθέσης. ᾿Αρχαιολογικό Μουσείο Θεσσαλονίκης, Athens 1985.

E. L. Smithson, *A Geometric Cemetery on the Areopagus: 1897, 1932, 1947*, Hesperia 43, 1974, pp. 325—390.

M. Sokołowski, *Muzeum Książąt Czartoryskich*, Kwartalnik Historyczny 6, 1892, pp. 229—276.

B. A. Sparkes, L. Talcott, *Athenian Agora 12: Black and Plain Pottery of the 5th and 4th Centuries B.C.*, Princeton, New Jersey 1970.

A. N. Stillwell, see *Corinth 15,2*.

J. Gy. Szilágyi, *Italo-Corinthiaca*, StEtr 26, 1958, pp. 273—287.

J. Gy. Szilágyi, *Remarques sur les vases étrusco-corinthiens de l'exposition étrusque de Vienne*, ArchCl 20, 1968, pp. 1—23.

J. Gy. Szilágyi, *Vases plastiques étrusques en forme de singe*, RA 1972, pp. 111—126.

J. Szymkiewicz, *Dział Sztuki Starożytnej w Muzeum Narodowym w Poznaniu (The Ancient Art Department of the Poznań National Museum)*, Studia Muzealne 14, 1984, pp. 29—47.

J. Śliwa, *Zur Geschichte der Antikensammlung an der Jagiellonen Universität*,

74

[in:] *Zur Geschichte der Klassischen Archäologie Jena—Kraków*, Jena 1985, pp. 54—66.

L. Talcott, see B. A. Sparkes.

J. P. Thalmann, *Céramique trouvée à Amathonte*, [in:] Gjerstad, *Geek Pottery*, pp. 81ff.

V. Tusa, *Ricerche e scavi nelle necropoli Selinunte*, ASAtene 60, 1982 (publ. 1984) pp. 189—202.

C. Tytgat, *Les materiel des tombes 121 et 135 d'Amathonte, 1—2*, Leuven 1978.

P. N. Ure, *Sixth and Fifth Century Pottery from Rhitsona*, Oxford 1927.

P. N. Ure, *Ring Aryballoi*, Hesperia 15, 1946, pp. 30—50.

Ure, AFR — P. N. Ure, *Aryballoi, Figurines from Rhitsona in Beotia*, Cambridge 1934.

P. N. Ure, see R. M. Burrows.

Vallet-Villard — G. Vallet, F. Villard, *Megara Hyblaea 2: La céramique archaïque*, Paris 1964.

E. Vanderpool, *The Rectangular Rock-cut Shaft*, Hesperia 15, 1946, p. 329ff.

M. N. Verdelis, *L'apparition du Sphinx dans l'art grec du VIIIe et VIIe S. av. J.C.*, BCH 85, 1951, p. 1ff.

K. Wallenstein, *Korinthische Plastik des 7. u. 6. Jahr. vor. Chr.*, Bonn 1971.

E. Walter-Karydi, *Samos 6: Samische Gefässe des 6. Jahr. v. Chr. Landschaftsstile Ostgriechischer Gefässe*, Bonn 1973.

S. S. Weinberg, *Remains from prehistoric Corinth*, Hesperia 6, 1937, p. 487ff.

S. S. Weinberg, *A Cross-section of Corinthian Antiquities (Excavations of 1940)*, Hesperia 17, 1948, p. 197ff.

S. S. Weinberg, see *Corinth 7, 1*.

C. K. Williams, *Corinth 1970: Forum Area*, Hesperia 40, 1971, p. 1ff.

C. K. Williams, *Corinth 1969, Forum Area*, Hesperia 39, 1970, p. 5ff.

R. S. Young, see *Corinth 13, 1*.

PLATES

PLATE I

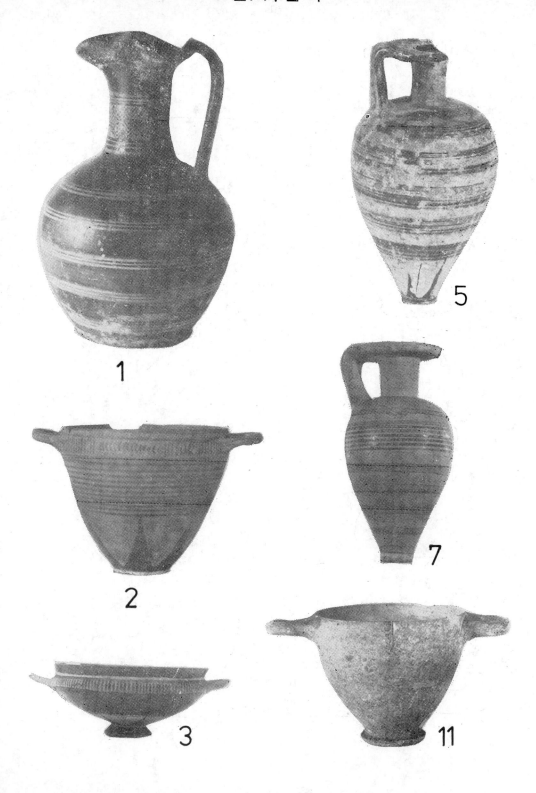

1

2

3

5

7

11

PLATE II

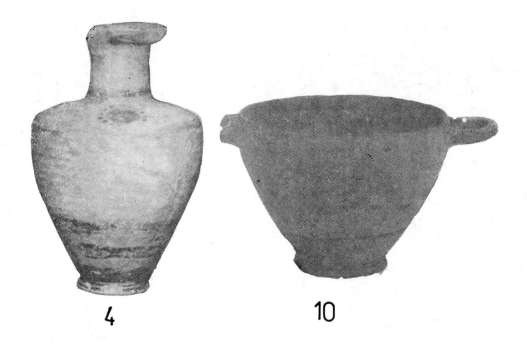

4

10

15

PLATE III

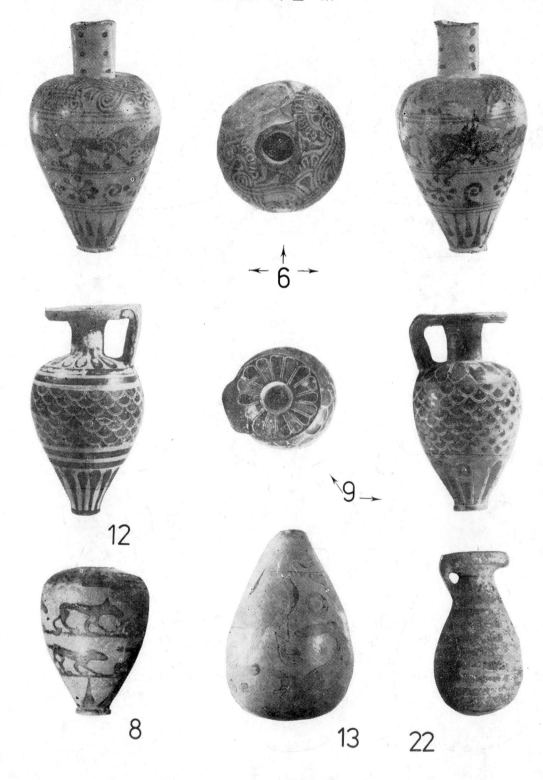

6

9

12

8

13

22

PLATE IV

← 14 →

16

23

18

21

20

19

PLATE VII

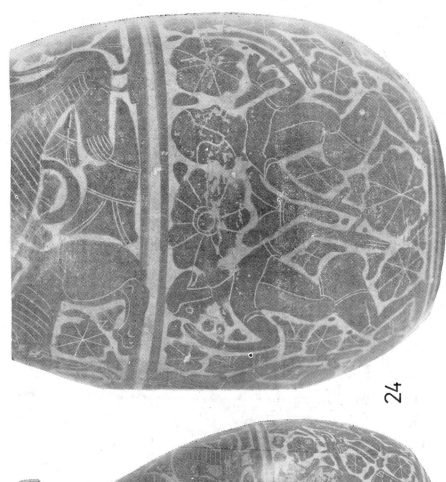

PLATE V

24

PLATE XII

35

PLATE XIII

39

PLATE XIV

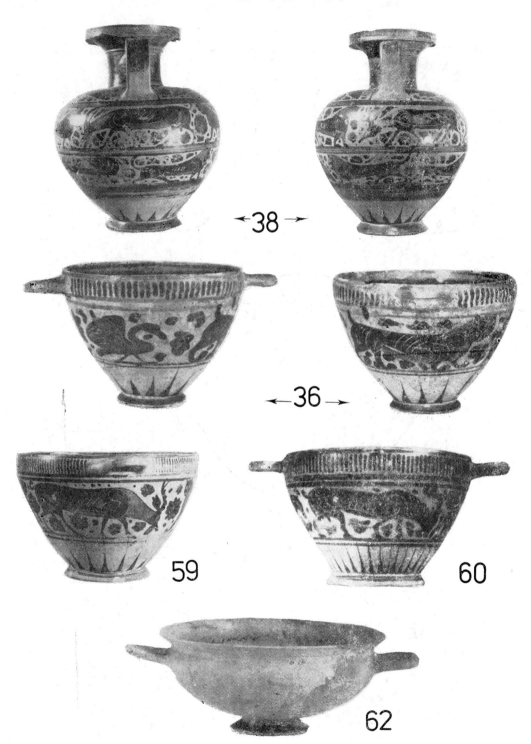

←38→

←36→

59

60

62

PLATE XV

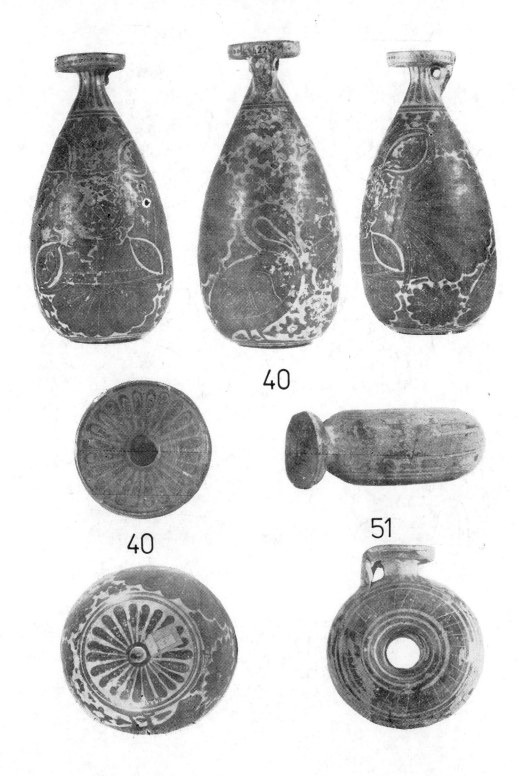

40

40

51

PLATE XVI

46

47

45

48

49

63

55

PLATE XVII

PLATE XVIII

52

57

PLATE XIX

53

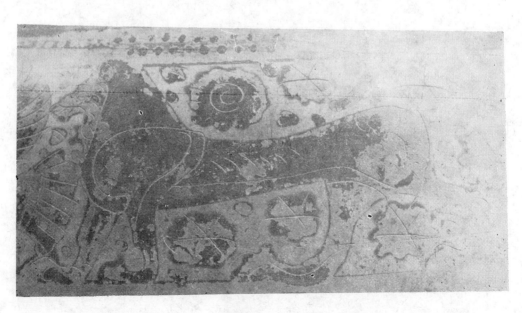

63

PLATE XX

54

PLATE XXI

54

56

PLATE XXII

58

61

PLATE XXIII

64

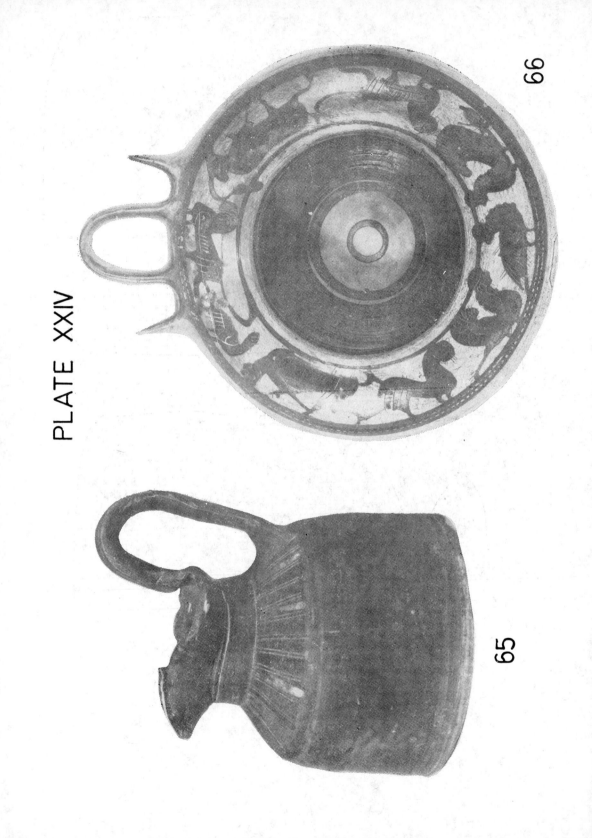

PLATE XXIV

66

65

PLATE XXV

67

PLATE XXVI

69

73

68

75

76

72

74

PLATE XXVII

70

77

71

PLATE XXVIII

79

78

PLATE XXIX

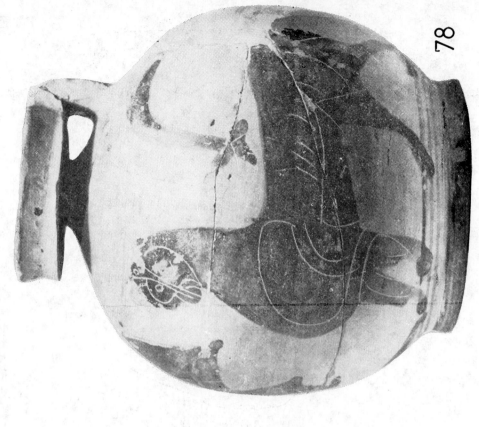

78

79

PLATE XXX

83

84

85

PLATE XXXI

80

81

82

86

87

← 89 →

PLATE XXXII

88

PLATE XXXIII

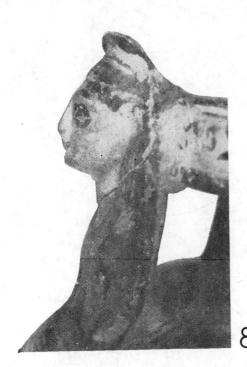

88

101

102

PLATE XXXIV

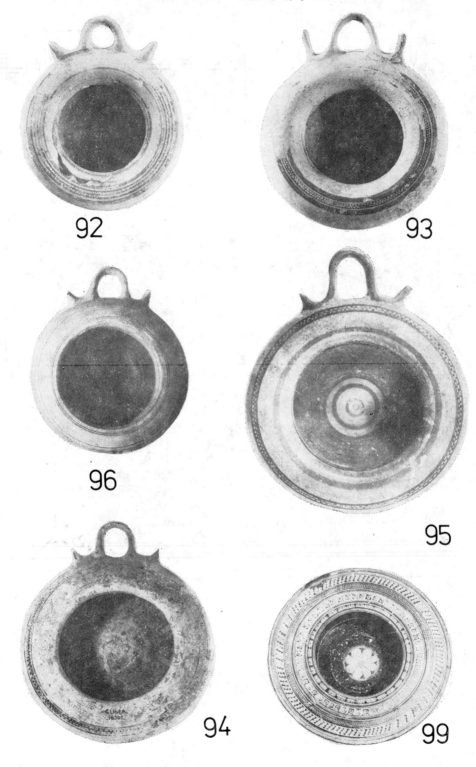

92

93

96

95

94

99

PLATE XXXV

93

92

96

95

97

99

97

98

PLATE XXXVI

100

90

91

103

112

104

105

PLATE XXXVII

106

108

110

107

111

109

PLATE XXXVIII

113

114

115

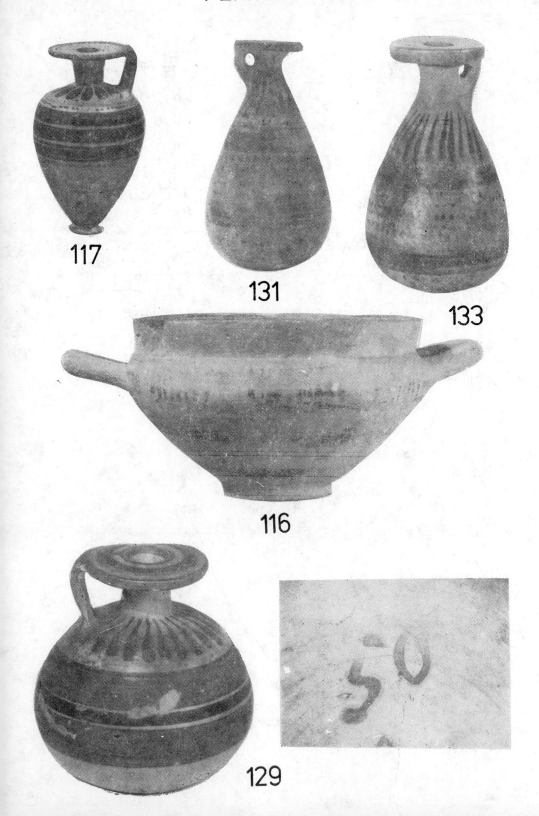

PLATE XXXIX

117

131

133

116

129

PLATE XL

118

119

122

120

121

123

125

124

PLATE XLI

126

130

136   134   135

127

132

128

PLATE XLII

PLATE XLIII

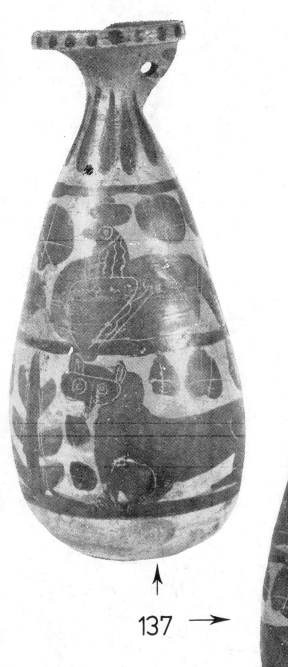

137

PLATE XLIV

138